CREATING
WOODEN
JEWELRY

CREATING
WOODEN
JEWELRY

24 SKILL-BUILDING PROJECTS AND TECHNIQUES

Sarah King

Fox Chapel
PUBLISHING
www.FoxChapelPublishing.com

For Jeff, Felix, and Emma

Fox Chapel Publishing Team
Vice President–Content: Christopher Reggio
Editor: Katie Ocasio
Jacket Designers: Llara Pazdan and Wendy Reynolds

Fil Rouge Press Ltd Team
Publisher: Judith More
Designer: Janis Utton
Photographer: Katherine Fawssett

ISBN 978-1-4971-0001-5

Library of Congress Cataloging-in-Publication Data

Names: King, Sarah, 1965- author.
Title: Creating wooden jewelry / Sarah King.
Other titles: Creating jewelry in wood
Description: North American edition. | Mount Joy, PA : Fox Chapel Publishing, 2019. | "Creating Wooden Jewelry is an Americanized edition of the book originally published by Fil Rouge Press Ltd under the title Creating Jewellery in Wood in the United Kingdom." | Includes bibliographical references and index. | Summary: "Contains information on skill-building projects and techniques for creating wooden jewelry. Includes step-by-step instructions and photographs for each project and technique discussed"-- Provided by publisher.
Identifiers: LCCN 2019023186 (print) | LCCN 2019023187 (ebook) | ISBN 9781497100015 (paperback) | ISBN 9781607657187 (ebook)
Subjects: LCSH: Woodwork--Amateurs' manuals. | Jewelry making--Amateurs' manuals. | Wooden jewelry.
Classification: LCC TT185 .K555 2019 (print) | LCC TT185 (ebook) | DDC 745.51--dc23
LC record available at https://lccn.loc.gov/2019023186
LC ebook record available at https://lccn.loc.gov/2019023187

To learn more about the other great books from Fox Chapel Publishing, or to find a retailer near you, call toll-free 800-457-9112 or visit us at *www.FoxChapelPublishing.com.*

We are always looking for talented authors. To submit an idea, please send a brief inquiry to acquisitions@foxchapelpublishing.com.

Printed in Malaysia
First printing

Contents

CHAPTER 1

Introduction

Foreword

ABOVE I developed the Oak Strata
Necklace on p. 142, adding a bio-resin setting
using the technique on p. 114.

Within this book, I have aimed to reflect the scope of the use of wood in contemporary jewelry. It is written very much from a jeweler's, rather than a wood specialist's, point of view.

For beginners, there are some easier projects, and for those with jewelry experience, there are ways of adding to the scope of your work with small additions to the usual hand tools. Large topics—woodturning, working with willow, gilding, and laminating—are just touched upon. All of these techniques could be explored and expanded into whole bodies of work. With a combination of imagination and exploration you can transform humble woods into striking pieces of jewelry.

Alongside the four studio jeweler profiles on pp. 56–9, 128–131, and 138–141, that show more examples of what can be achieved using wood, I urge everyone to research the list of wood jewelry makers' websites on p. 170, where you can find a wider range of wonderful work.

In my own practice, I work with wood, bio-resin, and precious metals to make sculptural, contemporary jewelry. Playing with spatial structures and sensual forms, they range from a relaxed, everyday collection to large transformative statement pieces. I

am interested in the visual qualities of different materials and the technical possibilities they allow.

My early work in silver was influenced by the work of the sculptor Constantin Brancusi, Japanese aesthetics, and African jewelry. Searching for contrasting materials to use in my work with which I could control the shaping led to experimentation with wood and resins, and I became a pioneer of the use of bio-resin in jewelry. Bio-resin is an eco material of sophisticated chemistry, made from sunflower seed oil. It doesn't have the yellow tinge of epoxy resin, which is important for my frosted clear pieces. I have replaced the exotic hardwoods I used in my early work, such as African blackwood, with woods such as ebonized oak and bog oak, as they are more local alternatives. I have often combined precious and non-precious materials such as wood and pearls, or silver with wood or bio-resin.

My solo Light Constructions exhibition held in Tokyo in 2003 began a new body of work in silver, white, and translucent bio-resin, and explored ideas of space and transparency, partly inspired by the artist Robert Ryman. The display was an installation creating a white world, with the pieces lit to accentuate their shadows. The jewelry was limited to rings and large bangles, often displayed in series of repeated shapes to focus on their sculptural and relative qualities. Some of the metal structures went on to be developed in silver and gold using laser-welding. Developing work for this book has led to a renewed interest in combining bio-resin, silver, and wood in new ways, in jewelry and some larger scale objects.

OPPOSITE A selection of rings in wood, silver, and bio-resin.

ABOVE Bio-resin pieces from my Light Constructions exhibition held in Tokyo.

The use of wood in jewelry

The new movement in jewelry in the 1970s questioned traditional values—the nature of preciousness and of jewelry as a symbol of wealth and status. With that came experimentation in techniques and a greater use of non-precious materials such as wood, acrylic, aluminum, and textiles. Influential figures within education in West Germany, Holland, and the UK were part of this movement, and new galleries opened to exhibit this new approach. American jewelers often had a more individualistic, narrative approach compared to European designers. Bruce Metcalf epitomizes this genre, and he continues to work in a wide range of materials including wood. Another key figure of the American scene was Marjorie Schick, whose striking "body sculptures" were constructed from painted wood elements.

It was within this atmosphere that Norwegian Liv Blåvarp started experimenting with laminated wood at the Royal College of Art in London in the 1980s, before returning to Norway where her work developed into smaller carved pieces joined together to have greater flexibility around the body. She is inspired by the Native American way of expressing feelings about nature. Some of her imagery is reminiscent of birds and animal anatomy. In her later work, there is a dynamic between internal and external forms, and all her pieces have integral solutions for their clasps.

Dutch jeweler Francis Willemstijn takes a poetic approach to materials that have historical resonance and personal significance. She used bog oak in her Heritage collection to make pieces reminiscent of *memento mori,* as bog oak was used in the 19th century as a substitute for jet. On a larger scale, British woodturner Eleanor Lakelin emphasizes the rhythm of growth, the eroding power of the elements, and the passing of time in her work. German jeweler Jasmin Matzakow has compared trees to humans, in that both have joints, skin/bark, and the ability for growth. Wood has been her primary material to explore jewelry, the body, and the social context of both, and she has gravitated toward woods closer to European traditions such as linden and spruce.

Other jewelers manipulate the physical properties of wood, for instance Dane Mette Jensen's steam-bent work and Japanese jeweler Manami Aoki's fiberized pieces. In recent years, digital technologies have been used for producing work, with British designer Anthony Roussel making early use of lasers for his laser-cut pieces. So the reasoning behind the choice of wood as a material for jewelry and the methods of its production continues to be very diverse.

LEFT Heart-shaped pin by Korean jeweler Dongchun Lee.

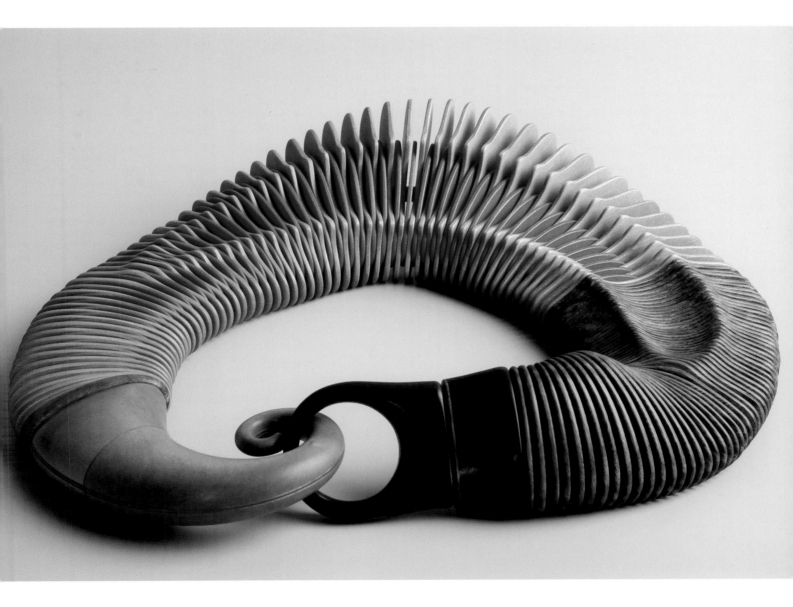

ABOVE *Where the Daisies Grow,* necklace in wood by Liv Blåvarp.

Choosing and using wood

The qualities and characteristics of different woods are a huge subject, and so I can only give a brief summary here. You will find a lot of information online or in specialty books on wood if you want to explore the topic further.

In choosing an appropriate wood for a particular project, your starting point should be the dimensions you will need and the technique you plan to use. It is also important to think through what finish you want—whether it will be painted or not. The choices can be rather overwhelming, so research the finishes used on similar techniques in wood jewelry and other applications, such as woodworker's projects, produced with similar techniques.

ABOVE This piece of horse-chestnut burr was used to create a pin that celebrates the wood's form, see pp. 96–101.

SUSTAINABILITY

The thoughtful sourcing of materials opens up new possibilities that also embody a more contemporary consciousness of sustainability issues. The perfect situation has to be that designer-makers are able to harvest their raw materials from their own trees. This is not possible for most people, but it is worth taking time to think about how you could source your materials from your own environment and having that as a starting point for your experimentation in wood.

Woods, especially tropical or exotic hardwoods, need to be carefully researched before deciding whether you can or want to use them (see Useful Information, p. 168). Wood suppliers are usually knowledgeable about their stock, so find sources that you trust and discuss any concerns you have. Another good approach is to find scraps from other processes that would otherwise be discarded. Consider using wood from old, larger wood objects that can be cut down or found-wood objects that can be reworked. Also, you may be able to collect your own green wood or driftwood.

TYPES OF WOOD AND THEIR CHARACTERISTICS
Hardwoods and softwoods

Softwoods are derived from conifer trees and tend to be found in cooler climates. They are cheaper and more porous than hardwoods and typically less strong (but not always, as yew is a softwood). Hardwoods are produced from deciduous trees, and are separated into two categories—temperate and tropical. The temperate hardwoods come from colder climates and tropical hardwoods are from the equatorial regions such as Africa, Asia, and South America. Hardwoods are denser than softwoods and more commonly used for jewelry, as they tend to be harder.

Manufactured woods

Plywood is made up of glued veneers, with each layer rotated 90 degrees to one another. MDF stands for *medium density fiberboard*. It is made of wood fibers compressed with resin; however, as it contains formaldehyde, it is regarded as an unappealing material.

LEFT Harvested driftwood. See p. 154 for ideas for making jewelry from wood found on the beach.

METHODS OF DRYING WOOD

The moisture content of wood needs to be changed before it is ready to use. This process is referred to as seasoning, and it needs to be done in a controlled way to prevent the wood from cracking. Wood is either air dried, which is the more traditional way, or kiln dried. Wood that hasn't been dried is referred to as green wood, and will need approximately one year of drying time per 1 in (25 mm) of thickness. When gathering your own green wood, you need to select larger diameter branches, as they will have more heartwood. See Terhi Tolvanen's profile on pp. 104–7 for further information on preparing green wood.

Heartwood and sapwood

Sapwood is the living wood where water is drawn up from the ground. As this becomes inactive, it will become central heartwood, and this is the wood that is usually used for woodwork, as it contains less water and will shrink less as it dries.

Wood grain and figure

A wood's grain is formed by the differing density of its growth throughout the year. A piece of wood will be stronger when you work with the grain as opposed to across it. Sanding should be done with the grain, and if you run your finger over the wood surface, it will feel smoother going with the grain than against it. The pattern within the grain of some woods is referred to as its figure, and is sometimes selected for visual appeal.

Hardness and toughness

The hardness of wood is measured in lbf, which stands for pound force. On the whole, jewelry does not have to withstand high impact, but the strength of wood you will need depends on the technique you are using and the scale of the finished piece. A wood's resistance to splitting is referred to as its toughness.

RIGHT Oak beads cut for use in the Oak Broken Line Necklace project on pp. 108–113.

MATCHING WOOD TO TECHNIQUE

Wood is a good material for making bold work, as it is light enough to allow large pieces to be worn with comfort. In addition, wood is very versatile in the number of techniques that can be used to shape it and the appearance it can be given with different finishes.

Carving: Basswood is a common initial choice for carving, as it is easy to work. Since it doesn't have a visible grain, it often tends to be stained or painted. Other hardwoods to try are sycamore, boxwood, cherry, oak, walnut, maple, apple, pear, and plum.

Woodturning: Both dry and green woods are suitable for turning, and there is a wealth of information and advice online from suppliers and enthusiasts.

Found objects: Most found objects will be made of hardwood (like the beech spoons used in this book on pp. 74–81) and, therefore, suitable for experimentation.

ABOVE I twisted locally sourced willow stems like these to make necklaces, earrings, and bangles—see pp. 42–9 for instructions.

ABOVE Think laterally when sourcing wood. Beech spoons, used for the necklace on p. 74, are easy to find at kitchen or hardware stores.

Inlay: Silver and pearls work well when contrasted to darker woods like exotic hardwoods. Try bog oak or a medium-color hardwood if you don't have a source of suitable scraps.

Laser-cutting: Only certain woods and plywood are suitable for laser-cutting. Laser-cutting companies often supply their own, so discuss with them the size of their wood, their laser-cutter bed, and your CAD drawing so that you know they're all compatible.

Veneers: Veneers, or thin slices of wood, are available in a wide range of wood types, and since they are often used as a surface layer for a less expensive material underneath, they are a very economical use of an expensive wood. Veneers are sometimes sold with an adhesive backing, but the project on pp. 68–9 uses a "raw" veneer product.

SOURCING

If you don't have access to a band saw, then you need to buy wood in a depth that is manageable to saw with whatever hand tools you have available. Wood suppliers will often slice down a larger piece of wood for a small fee. This is advisable since some woods can be very dense and hard to cut. It will be more cost-effective than buying many small pieces and there will be less waste if your wood is the right depth for what you need.

Search specialty websites for wood sold for certain types of work, such as guitar making and turning. For instance, guitar-makers tend to use attractive thin woods for the body of guitars, but there is waste from cutting the required shape and these scrap pieces can be bought. Lime is used for carving spoons and is, therefore, easy to find in suitably sized pieces. Model stores and lumberyards also sell useful woods. Fruit trees need pruning and might provide a good source of green wood if you have access to a garden tree or orchard.

MIXING WOOD WITH OTHER MEDIA

Jewelers working with wood don't always use it as a main medium, but as part of a mixed-media approach to their work. Often they will use whatever materials they feel convey a certain idea or feeling that is appropriate for a particular design. Many of the practical challenges of constructing pieces from materials without heating them, as you would solder metals to make attachments, apply to many non-precious materials.

Some plastics such as acrylic sheet can be sawn, drilled, and filed in a similar way to wood. For example, Emily Kidson uses laminating to attach Formica to wood and then adds the findings into the wood underneath. Care needs to be given not to damage the surface of plastics, but some can be polished on a motor polisher just by changing the mop and type of polish. Methods of construction such as riveting, glued pegs, plaque and claw settings, and threading would also be suitable to use for a wide range of materials. There are many contemporary jewelers who use a mixed-media approach, like Lucy Sarneel and Lisa Walker.

BREAKING THE RULES

Applying techniques from other disciplines, or, indeed, any influences from the world around us, can lead jewelers to experiment. Experimentation and chance are key to innovative results. If you only draw inspiration from other jewelers, it can be difficult to avoid making derivative work and harder to find your own voice or style. Sometimes having an in-depth knowledge of a certain field and the "correct" way of doing things can inhibit a fresh approach. For instance, Beppe Kessler's sewn balsa wood pieces came from her having a textile background and seeing what was possible across another material. It is also exciting to see a material used in an unexpected and hitherto unseen way. Manami Aoki soaks her wood then hammers the end grain until the fibers separate, and then sculpts it into tufts reminiscent of hair.

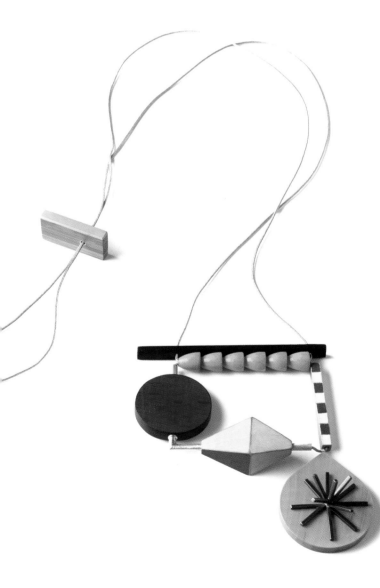

LEFT Mixed-media necklace by Katy Hackney
in wood, metal, colorcore, and nylon cord.

CHAPTER 2

Basic Techniques

Getting started

These two initial projects are designed as a starting point for the inexperienced jeweler and are also an introduction to wood for those who have previously worked in metal. The techniques may be simple, but this can make the design stage harder, since to make something striking from limited means can be harder than it initially appears. The dot pendant shown left also makes good use of shallow shaping, and might be another project to try at the beginner stage.

The step-by-step sequences for these projects are shown close-up from the first making stage, so it is important that you check out the workbench setup instructions you will need to carry out prior to this stage (see p. 159). When you are using a piercing saw or when you're filing, you will need to support your work on a bench peg that has had a V-shape cut into it. If you don't have a custom workbench with a bench peg built in, you can improvise with a bench peg clamped onto a table with a C-clamp. It is important to consider your setup here, because you will need to support the jewelry piece that you are working on, while at the same time, keeping your fingers from being in front of the piercing saw or the micromotor drill.

You also need to establish basic workshop safety. Keep any loose hair, necklaces, or scarves out of the way. Do not wear open-toe shoes in case you drop hot items or acid. Protect yourself from dust with a dust mask or respirator—this is especially important when doing jobs that toss up a lot of dust, such as when you are using a belt sander and when working with exotic hardwoods. Wear goggles whenever you are using machinery.

ABOVE Once you have mastered the techniques used in the projects in this chapter, try the dot pendant (see above and p. 120).

OPPOSITE See p. 174 for the index of difficulty for later projects like the spoon necklace, turned and gilded bangles, and ebony and pearl ring shown here.

TOOLS AND MATERIALS

- Pencil and cardstock
- Dividers
- Scalpel and cutting mat
- Walnut sheet, ³⁄₁₆ in (5 mm) from a model-making store; cut to 5½ x 4 in (140 x 100 mm)
- Standard piercing saw
- Fine wood saw blades
- Handheld drill or drill press, ¹⁄₁₆ in (1.5 mm)
- Dust mask and goggles
- 6¼-in (16-cm) half-round rough file
- 6¼-in (16-cm) half-round fine file
- Silver tube, ⅛-in (3-mm) outside diameter
- Cyanoacrylate glue and small piece of wire (to apply glue)
- Drill, ⅛ in (3 mm) in size, or ⅛-in (3-mm) ball burr
- Fine metal saw blades
- Sheet of 240-grit wet-and-dry paper
- Wax polish and paper towel (to apply it)
- Scissors
- Leather cord, 6½ ft long x ¹⁄₃₂ in thick (2 m long x 1 mm thick)

Walnut squiggle pendant

This first project helps you to practice basic techniques such as marking out, drilling, and working with a piercing saw. Using a spontaneous drawing technique with lots of cutouts gives the design lightness and liveliness. Keep it simple and bold.

OPPOSITE A doodle is translated into a dramatic wood shape suspended from a leather cord for this statement necklace.

1 Using a pencil and a piece of cardstock, draw some open squiggle shapes until you have one that you think will work well as a pendant. Make sure that the shapes that will be sawn out from the wood and discarded are not too small. You will need room to file the cut edges and small spaces are harder to file.

2 Set the dividers ¼ in (7 mm) apart and mark a parallel line to your squiggle on the cardstock. Use the divider point to mark dots, and then with a pencil, join them up and define the line.

3 Working on a cutting mat to protect your surface, use the scalpel to cut out your cardstock template.

4 With the pencil, draw around your template onto the wood.

5 Fit the piercing saw with a fine wood saw blade then cut along the outline of your pendant. You may find it easier to work in sections, sawing vertically down to the edge at intervals to make it easier to remove, rather than working around the outline in one pass.

6 Using the handheld drill and wearing a dust mask and goggles, drill several ¹⁄₁₆-in (1.5-mm) holes at intervals in the negative areas (the spaces that will be left empty) and thread your piercing saw though one of the holes (see step 5, p. 135). Making sure that your blade is taut, cut out the negative spaces.

7 Use a rough file, followed by a fine file, to smooth the edges.

8 Soften the sharp corners with a fine file, using sweeping strokes to polish the edge and make it look more finished.

9 Mark where you want to drill a ⅛-in (3-mm) hole for the silver tubing that will hold the leather cord. (In this design, two holes are drilled, one placed on each side of the squiggle's length.) Make sure that the holes aren't too close to the edge or the wood might be too fragile.

4

6

7

8

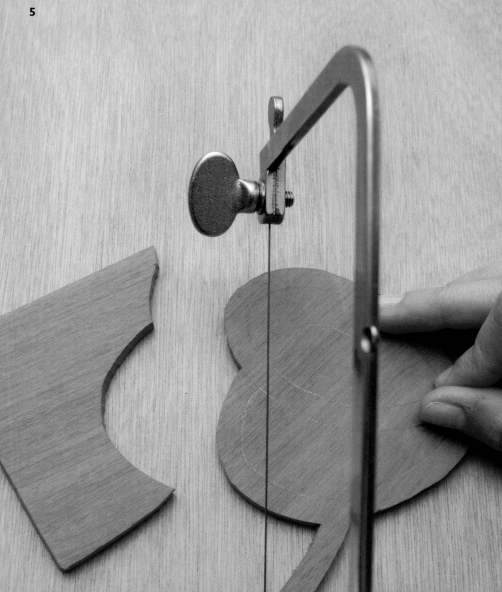

5

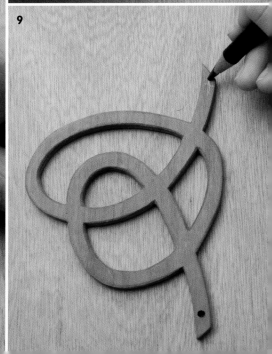

9

10

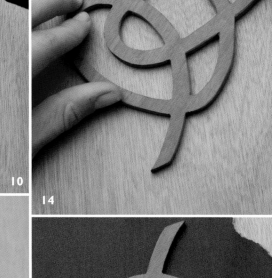

14

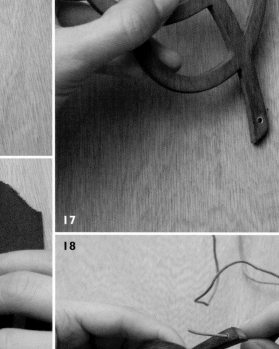

17

11

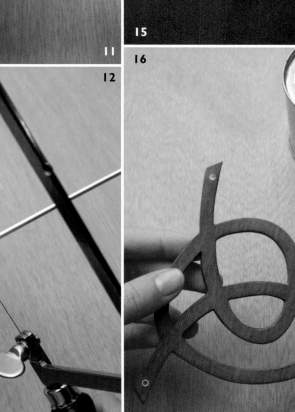

15

16

18

12

19

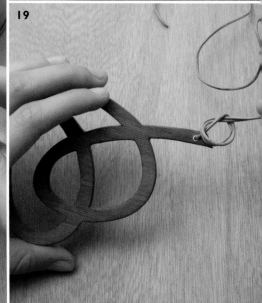

10 It is easier to make a straight hole with a small drill press, but it is also possible with a handheld drill. Holding your drill like a pencil, make a small ¹⁄₁₆-in (1.5-mm) hole where you have marked the cross, then use a ¹⁄₈-in (3-mm) burr to enlarge it.

11 Push the tube through the hole and out the other side. Put a small amount of cyanoacrylate glue on the end of a wire, dab it on the tube, then pull the tube back through the hole so that it is flush on one side. With this method the tube is less likely to stick than if you put the glue on first. Allow the glue to set.

12 With a piercing saw fitted with a fine metal blade, saw off the excess tube on the other side so that both sides of the tube are flush with the wood.

13 Repeat steps 9–11 on the second hole.

14 Using the fine file, file back the cut tubes flush with the wood surface.

15 Put the wet-and-dry paper flat on the bench and finish sanding the metal flush to the surface.

16 With a piece of paper towel, apply wax to the wood. Rub on and clean off any excess wax.

17 Using a ball burr, slightly round the inside edge of the tubes in order to make a nice highlight.

18 Thread your leather cord through the holes in the pendant.

19 Knot the cord above the tubes. Cut the remaining cord to your required length. Make a simple knot tie to close the necklace. Alternatively, affix cord end caps and a clasp to the ends of the cord.

tips for using a piercing saw

• Tighten the blade at one end and bend the frame together slightly by leaning your body on the frame against your bench. While the frame is bent together, tighten the other end and then release your pressure on the frame.

• Always make sure that the blade is taut: it must make a pinging sound when it is plucked.

• Never push the saw forward; keep the blade loose and concentrate on the vertical cut.

• Use long, sweeping strokes so that you are using the whole of the blade and not just the middle section.

• Make sure that you are holding the piece that you are sawing firmly in your other hand, as letting it tilt is the most common way to break the saw blade.

Undulating lime earrings

These earrings use a piece of wood that is deep enough to allow for some three-dimensional shaping. I have chosen basswood (also known as limewood) because it is quite soft, making it easier to work. However, that also means it can be easy to damage, so take care not to dent the wood in the later stages of making the earrings. As well as three-dimensional shaping, you will also learn how to make and attach silver findings (ear wires here), and how doing things in a counter-intuitive order can make this task easier.

OPPOSITE Shaped basswood is paired with custom-made silver findings to create softly sculptural earrings.

TOOLS AND MATERIALS

- Pencil, paper, and cardstock
- Scalpel and cutting mat
- Basswood, from a ⅜-in (10-mm)–thick slice
- Standard piercing saw
- Rough wax carving file
- Drill, ⅟₃₂ in (0.8 mm)
- Goggles and mask
- 240- and 1000-grit wet-and-dry paper
- Large ball burr, ¼–⁵⁄₁₆ in (6–8 mm) in a micromotor
- 3 solder bricks
- Small solder torch
- Easy solder paste
- 2 beads, ³⁄₃₂-in (2.5-mm), in silver
- Proprietary acid bath or heatproof glass dish and hot plate
- Acid for bath
- Brass tongs
- Round tool, ¼ in (7 mm)
- Rubber burr
- Fine file
- Silver polishing bit
- End cutting pliers
- Drill press or micromotor
- Parallel-action pliers
- Center punch, ¼ in (7 mm)
- Silver wire, ⅟₃₂ in diameter x 3¼ in long (0.8 mm x 8 cm)
- Silver cloth
- Cyanoacrylate glue
- White acrylic paint
- Small paintbrush and dish for finishing varnish
- Wax varnish in a clear, dead-flat finish

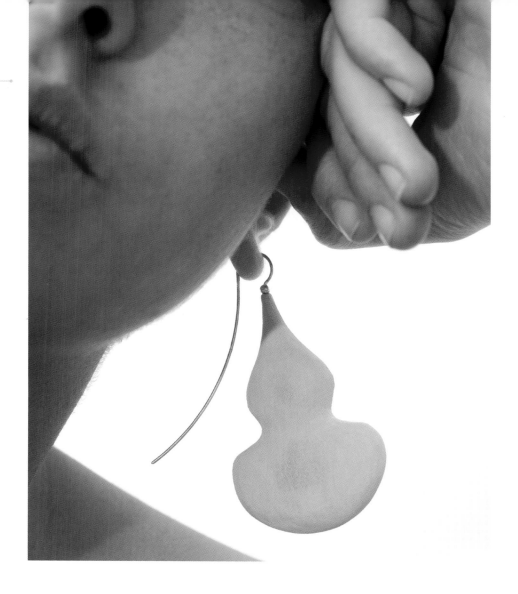

1 Make sketches until you are happy with the shape then, using a cutting mat, cut out the shape in cardstock with a scalpel. Hold this template up to your ear to check that you are happy with the design.

2 Draw around your cardstock template onto the ⅜ in (10 mm)–thick piece of wood, twice.

3 Saw around the shapes using a piercing saw, being sure to keep it vertical.

4 With a rough file, smooth the outside edges on both pieces.

5 On each shape, draw a pencil line to mark the middle of your edge.

6 Draw a pencil line to mark your highest areas on each shape.

7 Wearing goggles and mask, drill a ¹⁄₃₂-in (0.8-mm)–diameter hole approximately ³⁄₁₆ in (5 mm) deep in each piece where the ear wire will go. It is easier to do this now rather than once you have shaped the wood into a point. Make sure that you keep the drill held straight to the wood so the hole is vertical.

8 Using a large ball burr fitted on a hand-held micromotor, do some basic shaping.

9 Refine your shaping with the rough wax or wood file. Check how the file works on a scrap piece of wood first.

10 As you begin to get toward the end of the shaping, hold the pieces in your hand, as the wood can dent if held against a hard surface.

2

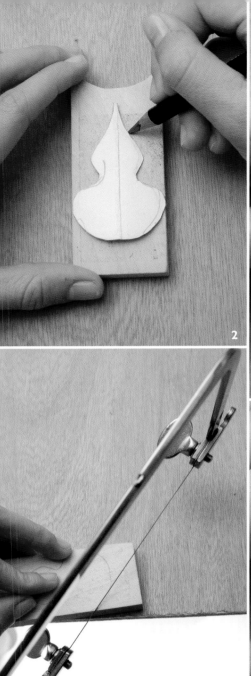

5

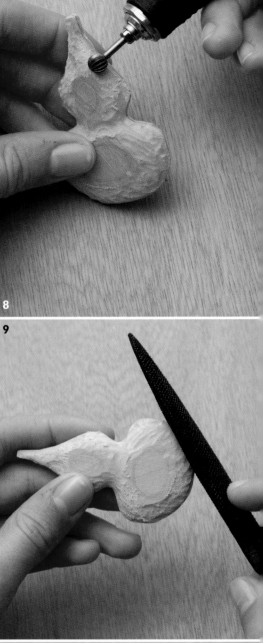

8

3

4

6

9

7

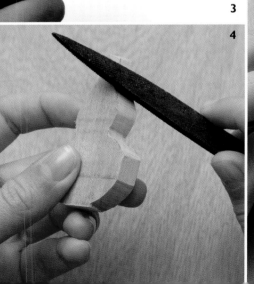

10

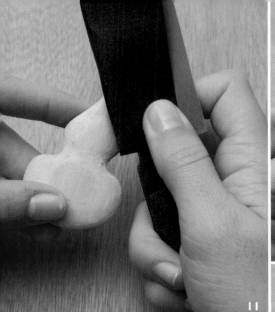

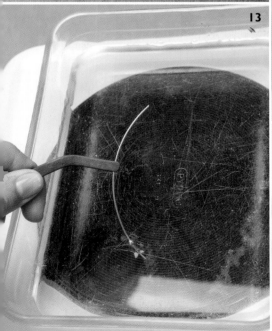

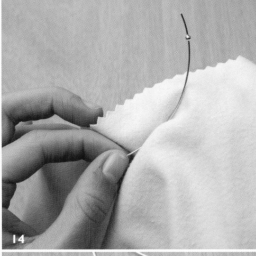

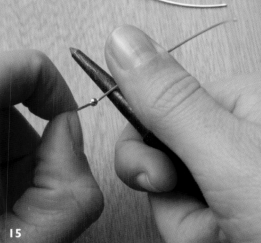

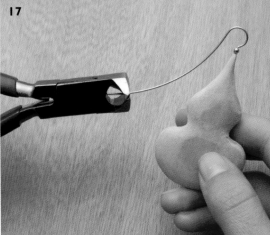

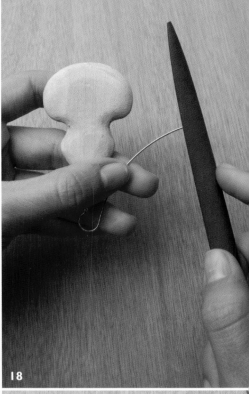

11 Using wet-and-dry paper wrapped around a file and handheld, sand over the surface.

12 To make the ear wires, cut the silver wire into two 1½-in (40-mm) lengths, set one cut length of wire on solder bricks, and, using the solder torch and paste, solder a ³⁄₃₂-in (2.5-mm) silver bead onto the end of the wire. Repeat with the second length.

13 Clean the ear wires in an acid bath, using brass tongs to insert and remove them (for safety instructions see p. 167).

14 Rub the wires with a silver cloth.

15 Using the parallel pliers, bend each ear wire directly above the bead and then around a round tool—approximately ¼ in (7 mm) round—to form the hooks.

16 Check the length of the wires in the hole in the wood part of the earring to ensure that the wire is hidden. Shorten if necessary to hide any excess wire, so that the bead sits directly on the top of the wood and any wire inside the wood below the bead is hidden. Glue in place.

17 Snip off the hook end of the ear wires to go through the ear as necessary, using the end cutting pliers.

18 Smooth the cut end of the silver hook wires using a fine file and a rubber polishing burr.

19 Polish the ear wires with a micromotor.

20 Paint the wood pieces with wax varnish mixed with just a small amount of white acrylic paint (to counteract yellowing). Test the color on a scrap first before painting the earring. Hang to dry on a length of cord, or in an earring holder, so that the wood remains untouched while it is drying.

making ear wires

· Ear wires are easy to make—your custom-made earrings deserve a handmade fitting rather than an off-the-shelf manufactured one

· Match your earring finding shape to your project. In the image above, a selection of variations is shown. Follow the steps 12–19 in this project to prepare your ear wires, bending them to your chosen shape.

CHAPTER 3

Shaping Wood

Exploring shaping techniques

This chapter introduces you to three-dimensional carving of wood, along with new projects that combine this carving technique with pegging a pearl into the top of a ring and doming silver sheet to make stud earring findings. I have also included further shaping techniques such as manipulating willow and cane, woodturning, shaping wood veneers, and carving cork.

The projects are designed to introduce you to a range of working methods and could all be used as a starting point for your own variations. The woodturning project is not a beginner's project and does presume previous experience and knowledge of woodturning. There are publications on the practicalities of making wood-turned jewelry you can consult, so I have concentrated on creating a design that will take you beyond those basics.

I chose to present a laminated veneers project as it requires less equipment than steam bending would, but they are both techniques that enable the manipulation of wood. Steam bending can be carried out without a steam box, but this would require experimentation with a microwave, damp clothes, and heat-resistant gloves.

ABOVE Wood bangle decorated with pearls, using the setting technique shown in steps 11–16 on p. 41.

OPPOSITE Ebony carved pendant and smaller silver version on a silver wire neckpiece, along with coordinating ebony, silver, and resin earrings.

TOOLS AND MATERIALS

- Ebony, ⅝ x 1½ x 1½ in (15 x 38 x 38 mm)
- White multi-surface paint marker or chinagraph marker
- Steel ruler
- Goggles and mask
- Band or piercing saw
- 3/0 wood saw blades, 5⅛ in (13 cm) long
- Handheld micromotor or drill press
- Drill bit, ¹¹⁄₁₆ in (17 mm)
- 6¼-in (16-cm) rough half-round file
- 6¼-in (16-cm) fine half-round file
- 240- and 1000-grit wet-and-dry paper
- Split pin
- Dividers
- Belt sander
- Ball burrs, ⅛ in (3 mm) and ¼ in (6 mm)
- Cylinder burr
- End cutting pliers
- Rifler file
- Silver wire, ¹⁄₃₂ x ⅜ in (0.8 x 10 mm)
- One-hole pearl, ⁵⁄₁₆-in (7.5 mm)
- Baby oil and paper towel
- Cyanoacrylate glue

Concave ebony and pearl ring

This ring introduces the technique of fully three-dimensional shaping. It uses a much harder wood than the earring project on pp. 26–31, and presents the challenge of accommodating a particular finger size. The technique of fitting a pearl down into a cup shows how to integrate a half-drilled stone into a wooden piece. You could use this method for any other type of jewelry, such as earrings (using the pegging technique from the laminated cuff links project on pp. 82–7), or a pendant using a pin (follow the method used for the ear wires in the basswood earrings on pp. 26–31, but make sure that the wire used for the pin is a bit thicker and pinned down a ⁵⁄₁₆-in [8-mm]–deep hole).

OPPOSITE Three-dimensional shaping of a small block of ebony creates a sculptural ring base that is then set with a single pearl bead.

1   With a white paint marker pen or chinagraph marker (grease pencil), and a steel ruler, mark a ⅝-in (15-mm)–long line on your length of ebony.

2   You can use a piercing saw with a wood blade to cut out a section of wood for your ring, but a band saw would be easier if you have access to one.

3   With a drill press, make a ¹¹⁄₁₆-in (17-mm) hole for the finger. Leave at least ³⁄₁₆ in (5 mm) between the hole and the edge of the wood. The hole can be placed anywhere on the wood as long as there is at least ³⁄₁₆ in (5 mm) between the hole and the edge of the wood.

4   Make sure that the ring fits the finger on which you wish to wear it. File the hole larger to fit with a rough round file, being sure to file the hole evenly all the way around and alternating which side you file.

5   Once you are happy with the size, smooth by filing with a fine, half-round file. If you have a micromotor, use a split pin with 240-grit wet-and-dry paper to even the surface of the ebony.

6   Using the dividers and the white marker pen or chinagraph marker, draw the design for the ring shape, measuring out from the hole. Sketch the overall shape on the side of the ring and saw it out with the piercing saw.

7   Mark guidelines on the top and sides of the piece using your paint marker pen.

8   Make the basic shape with a belt sander or rough file, or a large round burr in a handheld drill.

9

13

14

10

11

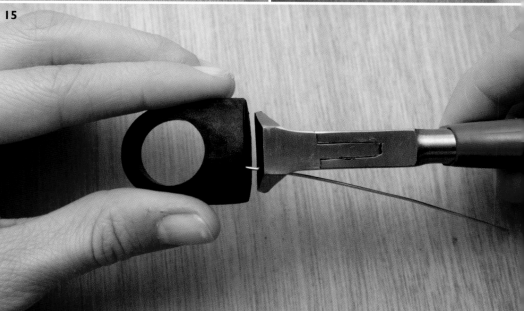

15

16

9 Once the excess material is removed, refine the shape with a rough file, followed by a fine file. Use a sheet of rough and then a sheet of fine 240-grit wet-and-dry paper wrapped around a file to get a good finish.

10 To practice the concave shaping on the top of the ring, saw out a practice piece from a wood scrap first. Draw a line to mark the middle line. Use the large ¼-in (6-mm) ball burr (left) to remove the wood. Then define the middle line with the ⅛-in (3-mm) burr (middle), followed by the edge of the cylinder burr (right), to get a crisp line. Use the rifler file (far right) to even out the two sloping sides. Once you are happy with your methods, repeat this step with the actual ring.

11 Mark where you want the middle of the pearl and drill a ¹⁄₃₂-in (0.8-mm) guide hole approximately ⁵⁄₃₂-in (4 mm) deep (depending on the height of your ring).

12 Using the small hole as a guide, drill out a large cup-shaped hole with the ¼-in (6-mm) ball burr, checking as you go until you are happy with how the pearl sits in it.

13 Re-drill the ¹⁄₃₂-in (0.8-mm) hole in the middle of the dip if necessary, and glue the silver wire down the hole. I have used twisted wire, but plain silver wire would work, too.

14 Dab a little baby oil on a piece of paper towel to finish the wood. Doing it at this stage will prevent the oil from touching the pearl.

15 Use the end cutting pliers to trim the wire to the correct length.

16 Glue the pearl onto the wire using the glue application technique (see steps 9–10 on pp. 122–5). You need the glue to be inside the hole of the pearl, but not so much that it shows once the pearl is pushed down onto the ring. Your pearl should sit down neatly into the cup shape. Leave the glue to set.

Twisted willow and cane sets

I combined plant material with metal to create these sets—a bangle and earrings made from twisted willow, and a necklace, earrings, and bangle set made from cane, all with custom-made silver findings. I explored willow and cane for this project, but there is also room to experiment with garden plants. Willow is usually used for larger-scale basketry, constructed by holding green or soaked lengths in tension and allowing them to dry out. You will find that when willow is used on a smaller scale, as here for jewelry, it is prone to kinking. After some experimentation with different lengths and varieties, I chose a stripped willow (*Salix purpurea*). The project also reveals the malleability of silver as a cold connection since the annealed silver is closed around wood to form silver findings.

TOOLS AND MATERIALS

- Stripped willow, 3 ft (1 m)
- Ruler
- Snips
- Square-section silver wire, 4 x 1/16 in (100 x 1.5 mm), for the necklace findings
- Square-section silver wire, 3/32 x 4¾ in (2.5 x 120 mm), for the bangle findings
- 2 lengths of 1/32-in (0.8-mm) silver wire, 3/8 in (10 mm) each, for the earring posts
- Solder torch
- Solder bricks
- Solder paste
- Piercing saw
- Metal sawblades
- 2 pairs of parallel pliers, or a vise and one pair of parallel pliers
- 2 punches, 5/16 in (9 mm) and ¾ in (18 mm), or similar objects to wrap around
- Acid bath
- Cyanoacrylate glue
- Wax varnish in a dead flat finish (alternatively, microcrystalline wax)
- Earring butterfly backs

OPPOSITE Twisted cane necklace and bangle, and three sizes of hoop earrings. Both natural and painted finishes are used.

WILLOW VERSIONS

1 Soak the willow in water overnight to soften it. Have extra lengths soaked to allow for wastage. For the willow part of the bangle, choose either two or three ⅛-in (2–4 mm)–diameter lengths.

2 Hold the thicker end (the butt) of the willow in your left hand and soften the fibers by running the thumb of your right hand along the length in a curved motion.

3 To make the willow bangle base, form an 3-in (80-mm)–diameter loop and bend the willow under and up through the circle. The willow rod needs to be handled gently to avoid kinking. If it does kink, then you need to discard it and use another length.

4 Repeat the loop around your circle until you come to the end of the length.

5 Add in new lengths until your bangle is as wide as you want it to be and fits well over the hand, about 2¾ in (70 mm) of inside diameter.

6 Snip the ends and leave to dry.

7 For the willow section of the earrings, use the same method as employed for the bangle in steps 1–6, but instead use one ¹⁄₃₂–⅛-in (1.5–3-mm)–diameter length. Start with a loop that is 1¾ in (4.5 cm) in diameter. For this size, a single length of willow will probably be sufficient.

8 Repeat to make a second hoop the same size and leave to dry.

9 To prepare the wire for the twisted silver hoop-shaped findings, place it on solder bricks and use the solder torch to heat all the wire until it is cherry red to anneal it and make it soft enough to twist. Quench in cold water.

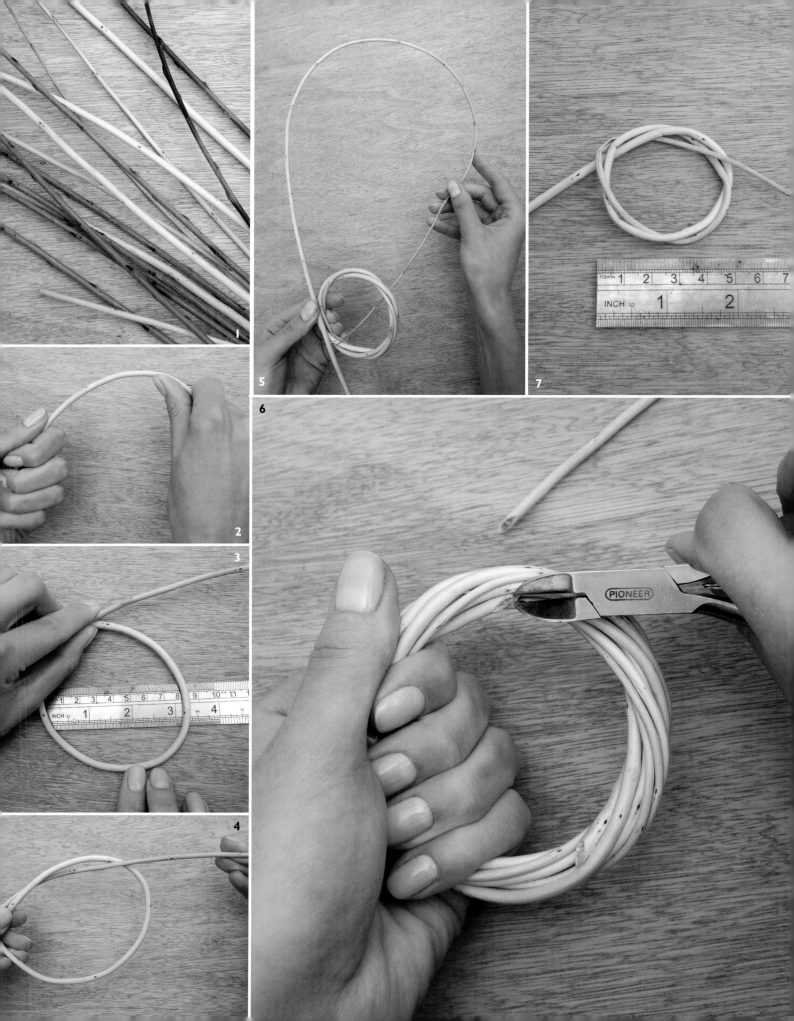

10 To make the silver hoop findings for the bangle, use the 3/32-in (2.5-mm) silver wire. Clamp one end in a vise or in parallel pliers. Holding the other set of parallel pliers in your right hand, twist a quarter rotation. Repeat, working your way back along the wire. The gap in between your twists will relate to how close the twists are in the silver.

11 Anneal (heat to soften) your twisted length of 3/32-in (2.5-mm) silver wire again using the solder torch, and wrap it around the 3/4-in (18-mm) punch until as much of the wire is coiled as possible.

12 Pull the silver coil off the punch and clean it in the acid bath.

13 Using a piercing saw, cut through the silver rings you have formed. Some people like to saw from the outside, while others like to thread the blade through the rings and saw from the inside. Whichever method you prefer, make sure that you start and finish the job in one place or you will have saw cuts in your finished rings.

14 To make the silver earring findings, anneal and twist the silver wire in the same manner as the bangle ones (see steps 9–12). The 1/16-in (1.5-mm) wire is coiled around a 5/16-in (9-mm) punch.

15 Once you have finished the two smaller rings, flatten them using the parallel pliers so they will sit flat on the solder bricks.

16 Solder the two 3/8-in (10-mm) lengths of silver wire that form the earring posts onto the two smaller rings, holding the wires in reverse-action tweezers.

17 Clean the silver findings in the acid bath.

18 To finish the willow, using a very small amount of glue on a piece or wire or broken sawblade, gently lift any snipped ends of willow on the bangle and hoops and carefully glue them down.

19 Use a paintbrush to cover all the willow parts with wax varnish and leave to dry thoroughly. It can be helpful to hang them on a small hook or on some fine thread to avoid disturbing the varnish too much as it dries.

20 Rub the silver findings with a silver cloth to polish them.

21 Attach the silver parts to the twisted willow bangle, and then attach the earring hoops, using both pairs of parallel pliers to help you line up and close the two sides of the jump rings.

22 Attach the butterfly backs to the earrings.

10

14

11

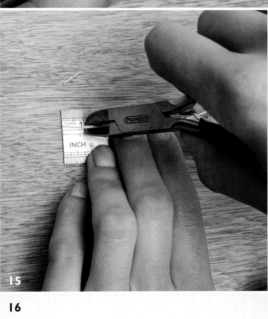

15

19

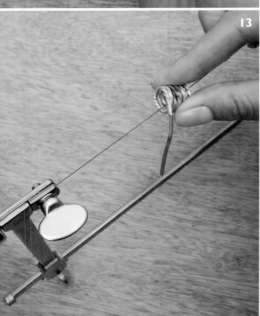

13

16

21

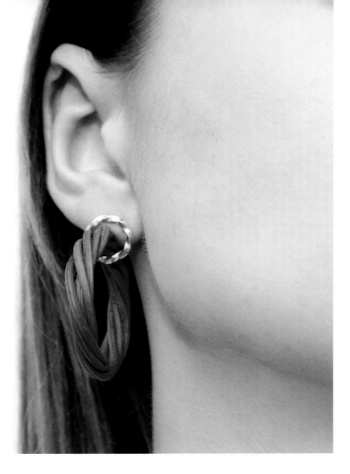

TOOLS AND MATERIALS

TOOLS AND MATERIALS

- For the cane versions:
- 11½ ft (3.5 m) of ⅛-in (3-mm) cane
- 31½ in (80 cm) of ⁵⁄₆₄-in (2-mm) cane
- 47 in (120 cm) of ¹⁄₁₆-in (1.5-mm) cane
- 4¾ in (12 cm) of ³⁄₃₂-in (2.5-mm) square-section silver wire, for the bangle findings
- 2 lengths of ¹⁄₃₂-in (0.8-mm) silver wire, ⅜-in (10-mm) each, for earring posts
- Acrylic paint
- All-purpose dye
- Microcrystalline wax
- Parallel pliers
- Solder torch
- Solder bricks
- Punch, ¾ in (18 mm)
- Acid bath
- Piercing saw
- Metal saw blade
- Reverse-action tweezers

CANE VERSIONS

If you don't have the patience to carefully coax willow into smaller circles, then I have also provided instructions for a cane version of this design that is much easier to make. The cane is actually a rainforest-grown vine and is more malleable. It can be bought with a consistent circumference, making it much easier to work.

1 Cane only needs one hour's pre-soaking, but it dries out quickly so take it out of the water as you need it.

2 Measure and cut your cane. For the bangle, I used 11½ ft (3.5 m) of ⅛-in (3-mm) cane. While for the earrings, I used 31½ in (80 cm) of ⁵⁄₆₄-in (2-mm) cane, and 47 in (120 cm) of ¹⁄₁₆-in (1.5-mm) cane.

3 Wind the cane for the bangle around an initial loop of 3 in (8 cm). For the smaller earrings, wind around a 1½-in (4-cm) loop, and for the larger earrings, wind the cane around a 2¼-in (6-cm) loop.

4 Dye the red earrings using an all-purpose dye.

5 For the necklace, which is formed entirely of cane hoops with no silver parts, I played around with ¹⁄₁₆-in (1.5-mm) and ⁵⁄₆₄-in (2-mm) cane, using differing diameter starting points for the individual hoops. First, make the larger hoops and paint them yellow. Next, link them together with the smaller hoops.

6 I used a yellow acrylic paint to color the cane.

7 Follow the directions in steps 8–16 of the willow project to make the silver parts. To attach them, follow step 21 in the willow project (see p. 46).

8 Finally, seal all the cane pieces. For any colored surfaces, use microcrystalline wax; otherwise, use the same wax varnish as the willow (see step 19 on p. 46).

TOOLS AND MATERIALS

- Carving wax
- Carving wax file
- Circles template
- Belt sander (optional)
- Piercing saw and wax saw blade
- Pencil and paper
- Dividers and ruler
- 2 pieces of spalted beech, ⅜ x 1 x 1 in (10 x 25 x 25 mm)
- Dust mask and goggles
- Sheet of 240-grit wet-and-dry paper
- Disc cutter
- 1½-in (40-mm) length of ⅟₃₂-in (0.8-mm) silver wire
- Silver sheet, ⅟₃₂ in (0.8 mm) thick, approx ⅝ x 1½ in (15 x 30 mm)
- Doming block
- Punch
- Metal hammer
- Micromotor
- Drill bit, ⅟₃₂ in (0.8 mm)
- Rough file
- Smooth file
- End cutting pliers or snips
- Fine-point marker
- Solder torch and bricks
- Solder paste
- Acid bath
- Microcrystalline wax
- Cyanoacrylate glue or two-part epoxy glue
- Extra-large butterfly earring backs

Spalted beech saucer stud earrings

This simple project shows one way to make stud earrings using a doming block. The simplicity of the design also allows the natural patterning within woods to take center stage. I chose to use spalted beech, which has random patterning caused by a fungus. The small length of wood I bought for this project was sold by a woodturning supplier, and would typically be used to make knife handles. Until you have shaped your pieces, you can't be sure quite how the pattern will show up or relate to the overall shaping of the piece, so there is an element of surprise and each earring you make will be different.

OPPOSITE Spalted beech stud earrings with handmade findings in silver.

1   To find pleasing proportions for different shapes, create models. These models are made from carving wax cut with a with a wax blade on a piercing saw, and then shaped by a wax file. I used this test method on a 1-in (25-mm) diameter circle. I planned on using as much of my wood as possible.

2   Use the dividers to mark a ⅜-in (10-mm) line around your wood.

3   With the piercing saw, cut off two ⅜-in (10-mm) beech slices. You might need to cut several to choose the two that have interesting markings and work as a pair.

4   Using a template or dividers, draw a 1-in (25-mm) circle on each piece of wood.

5   Saw out the shape with a piercing saw, being careful to keep your saw vertical or it will distort the underside of your circle. Use the rough file to refine the cut edge.

6   Mark the middle line of the edge of the wood shapes with a pencil.

7   Use a rough file or a belt sander to dome either side of the wood shapes up to the marked line.

8   Once you are happy with the overall shape of the wood parts, refine them with a fine file and wet-and-dry paper.

9   Seal the wood with microcrystalline wax and leave to dry.

10 Use the disc cutter and a mallet or metal hammer to stamp out two ½-in (12-mm) silver discs.

11 Mark the middle point of the silver discs using the fine marker pen.

12 Drill a ¹⁄₃₂-in (0.8-mm) hole in each disc, then cut two ¾-in (20-mm) lengths of ¹⁄₃₂-in (0.8-mm) silver wire.

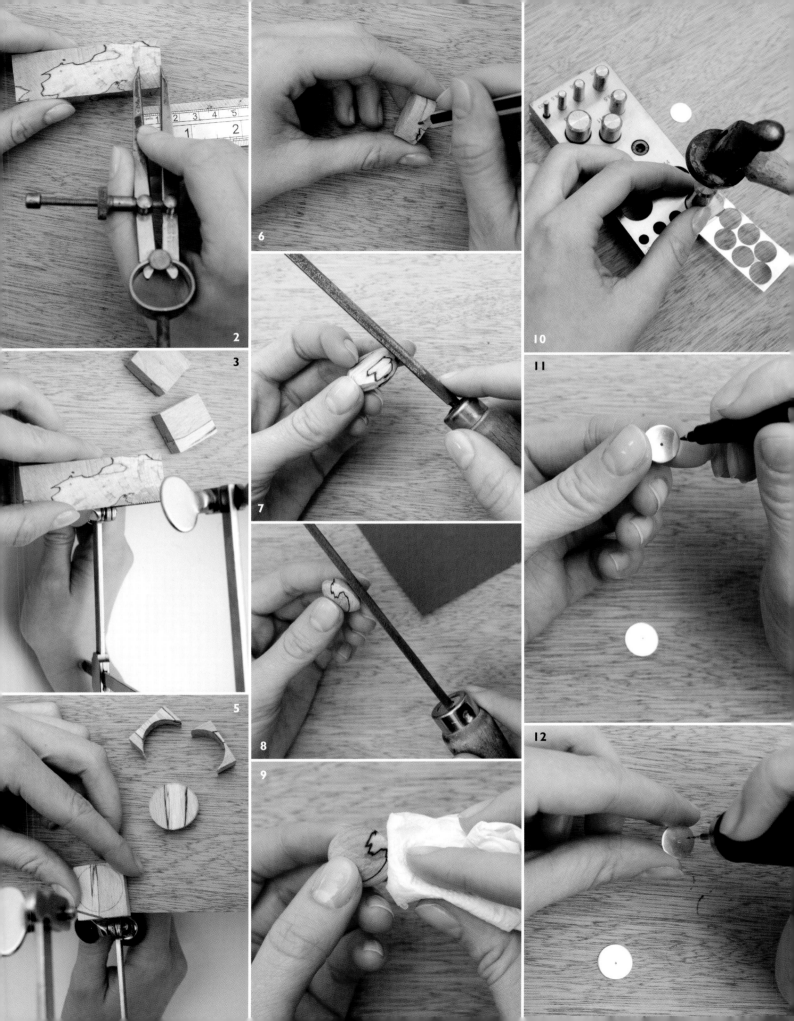

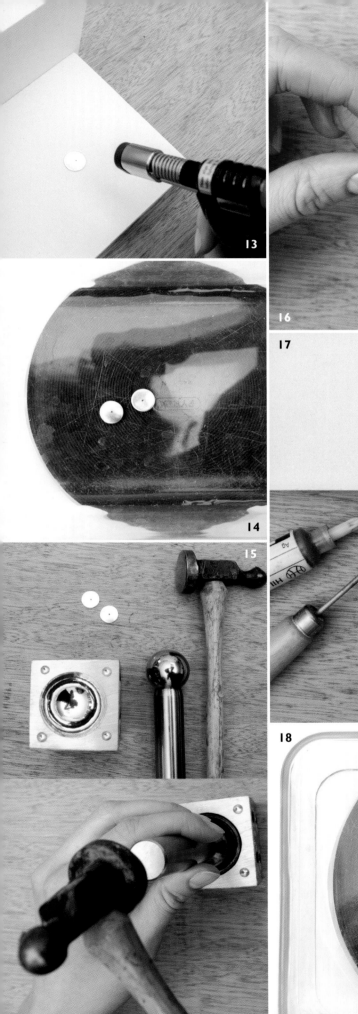

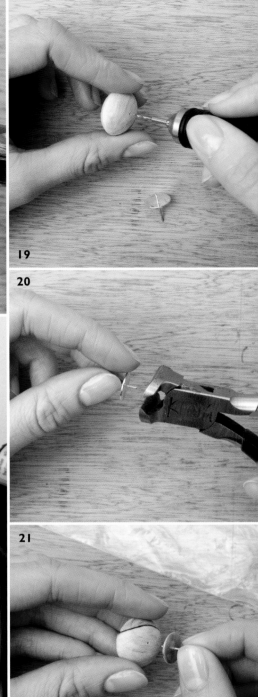

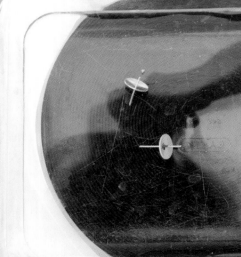

variations

- Other woods with interesting grains: try Zebrano, birdseye maple, rosewood (careful sourcing is necessary for tropical hardwoods such as rosewoods), or Brazilian lacewood.

- Alternative surface decoration: use a plainer piece of wood such as lime, and try some of the painted surface effects from p. 149.

- Inlays: try some of the alternative inlays on p. 125.

- Alternative domed finding: a deeper dome was used to make a pendant finding for the nicely shaped piece of driftwood above. I soldered a ⅟₃₂-in (0.8-mm) wire on the inside. Then I turned it upside down, with the wire held in-between two solder bricks, to solder on the jump ring.

13 Anneal (heat to soften) the discs using a solder torch against solder bricks.

14 Clean in the acid bath. You do not want impurities hammered into the surface of the silver when you dome them.

15 Using a large punch in the doming block, hammer the discs into a shallow dome that fits into the gentle dome of the wooden parts.

16 Thread a silver wire halfway through the hole in each disc.

17 Solder the wire into place with a small amount of solder paste in the concave side of the disc.

18 Having cleaned all the silver parts in the acid bath, rub them with a silver cloth.

19 Drill a ⅟₃₂-in (0.8-mm) hole in the middle point of the wood, making it about ³⁄₁₆ in (5 mm) deep.

20 Using end cutting pliers, trim the silver wire so that the silver dome finding sits flush on the wood.

21 Glue in the silver wire with cyanoacrylate glue or two-part epoxy glue.

22 When the glue is dry, add large butterfly earring backs to the wire posts.

Inni Parnanen

Finnish jewelry artist and designer Inni Parnanen graduated as a goldsmith from Lahti Institute of Design in 1995 and completed her Master's Degree in the Department of Design of the University of Art and Design, Helsinki, in 1998. She actively participates in exhibitions both in Finland and internationally. Her works can be found in many international publications as well as in private and public collections.

ABOVE Plywood is bent into loops for these bracelets made of overlapping folds.

ABOVE A simple bent twist is the key to
these plywood bangles.

What are the main themes of your work?

I explore structures and materials, and I find the wide variety of
possibilities that jewelry as a medium provides very engaging.
The materials I choose as my starting point are often selected
randomly, but those materials essentially guide me through
the process. The nature of the material and the structure of the
resulting piece define how my jewelry is worn.

*Are there artists or other influences that have been particularly
important to your development?*

When it comes to use of material, I find traditional craft very
inspiring. Artists that use tradition with an interesting twist,
such as for example designer couple Aamu Song and Johan
Olin, whose work I truly admire. Also artist Janna Syvänoja´s

work has been important to me. Her way of using materials is
breathtaking.

*Your jewelry has used different materials such as parchment,
horn, silver, and wood. Has the work in one material led to you
making new work in another material?*

I have a curiosity for materials and often one thing leads to
another. The technique applied to different kind of materials can
be the same. What happens when the material changes is the
essential discovery, as well as how the technique used acts with
the shape and structure.

*Can you describe your working process—drawing, model-
making, etc.—and how it varies with the different areas of your
work?*

I work with three-dimensional sketches and most often I start
with paper models. Often, I make a full-size prototype too.

ABOVE A quartet of plywood *Pallo* necklaces, with magnetic fastenings.

LEFT A reversible design in plywood, that can be worn as a neclace or bracelet.

OPPOSITE Plywood flowers are linked by silver rings and the resulting piece fastened with a linen ribbon.

*What techniques do you use to create your wood pieces—
how much are you using Cad Cam laser-cutting or hand-
construction?*

The use of material guides the process, and feeling one's way
forward by hand is crucial, but laser-cutting is an important
tool, and in many ways, it has also been an enabler for many of
my processes. With plywood, I use also heating, pressing, and
bending.

*The woods you use are thin and fragile, thin plywood, birch bark,
and, presumably, suit both your ideas and techniques?*

I find the contradictions in my work very interesting. While the
piece looks complex, it is extremely simple in structure. The
structures look organic yet they have a geometrical
starting point. The contrast of simplicity and
complexity, sensitivity and hardness
is a constant source of inspiration.
Plywood is a diverse material
which suits my purposes. Although I
do not wish to be bound by using only
certain kinds of materials, I find myself
drawn to natural materials and their
surprising features. When working
with plywood, I use several
methods to bend it. And, [since] I
don't have a steaming machine,
I soak the material before
bending. Sometimes I use a hot-
air blower. I test a lot, and the
right method comes in time.
There are several different
types of plywood and I´ve
noticed that all of them have
slightly different features. So when I
increase the size of a piece, for example, I
come up with a problem that has to be solved.

*What has drawn you to start working
on a larger scale?*

As I find that the use of material leads my process,
it has also led me fluently into works with larger scale. The
structures in my work grow larger very naturally. The variation
in size has also become part of the inspiration.

Do you see your work as part of a Nordic tradition?

I find my work very much part of Nordic tradition. My interest
in the natural world and craftsmanship has a strong connection
with Finnish modernism. I am also both process- and product-
driven.

How do you balance ideas and practical concerns in your work?

The technical issues are solved while working. As most of my
work is based on a certain structure, technical solutions are the
backbone of my work, and often, also the things that I start with.

TOOLS AND MATERIALS

- Digital or regular drawing of design
- Sycamore bowl blank, 5 x 3 in (127 x 76 mm)
- Power drill
- Bench lathe
- Turning helmet (safety helmet especially for woodturning)
- Wood screws (to attach faceplate)
- Tape (any tape to wrap around the drill bit to mark the length to drill into wood)
- Calipers
- Ruler
- Modified chisel
- Gouge, ⅜ in (10 mm)
- Skew chisel
- Flat chisel
- 600- and 240-grit wet-and-dry paper
- Split pin
- Micromotor
- Rounding-off bits, ⅜ in (10 mm) and 1 in (25 mm)
- Microcrystalline wax or varnish of your choice

Sycamore asymmetric bangle

This bangle is turned on a bench lathe using a blank sold pre-prepared for turning a bowl. Don't attempt woodturning without special training as it can be dangerous. Making something that doesn't need the central part hollowed out would be an easier project for those new to woodturning. This asymmetric design can be worn stacked in different directions, forming interesting shapes. The design was drawn up into a digital drawing to make it easier to follow beside the lathe. This bangle is 1½ in (40 mm) wide, with an inside diameter of 2½ in (65 mm). The depth of the wood is ¾ in (20 mm) and the highest point is ½ in (14 mm) from one edge, leaving 1 in (25 mm) for the concave sloping. The bottom of the slope is left $5/_{32}$ in (4 mm) thick.

OPPOSITE Turned sycamore bangle finished with microcrystalline wax.

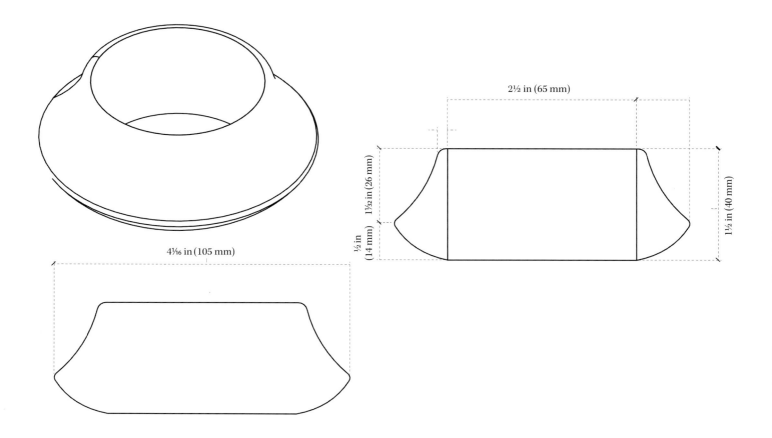

2½ in (65 mm)

1¹⁄₃₂ in (26 mm)

½ in (14 mm)

1½ in (40 mm)

4¹⁄₁₆ in (105 mm)

1 Using your drawing as a guide, mark the middle of the wood.

2 Attach the faceplate to the wood with a power drill and wood screws. Care and thought must be given at this stage to the position and depth of the screws, or their holes will be visible in the final piece.

3 Attach the faceplate to the lathe, making sure that the tool rest doesn't hit the wood as it spins.

4 Carve an indentation with a skew chisel that is sufficiently small for the chuck to grip, and remove the faceplate.

5 Reattach the wood you are turning to the lathe using the chuck.

6 Using the ruler, calipers, and a round point, measure and mark the overall width of the bangle 4 in (105 mm) to the side of the wood. Take the wood down to the line where you used the calipers and round point in order to make an indentation to mark the wood.

7 Wrap tape on the ⅝-in (16-mm) drill that is attached to the right-hand side of the lathe. This helps guide how deep the central hole should be in order to hollow out the central 2½-in (65-mm) diameter of the bangle.

8 Remove the center of the wood with a modified chisel, a gouge, and then a skew chisel, making sure that the inside diameter is consistent all the way in. Left to right in middle far-right photo: modified chisel, gouge, skew chisel, flat chisel, long chisel.

9 Now that the inside hole is done, work on the outside to take the bangle thickness down to ¾ in (20 mm) with a skew chisel and a flat chisel.

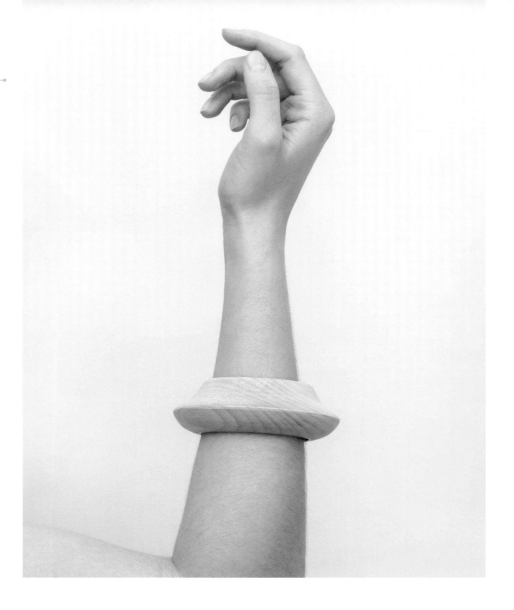

10 Add the outside width markings again with calipers and a ruler. There will be a line ½ in (14 mm) from the right-hand side and a line 1½ in (40 mm) from that edge, marking where the other edge of the bangle will be.

11 Take off the convex curve with the larger round-off bit followed by the skew chisel.

12 Take the sharpness off the inside edge of bangle with the skew chisel so that the bangle will be comfortable to take on and off.

13 Take down the spare wood to the left of the bangle using a rounding-off bit.

14 Shape the concave slope with a ⅜-in (10-mm) gouge, followed by the ⅜-in (10-mm) rounding-off bit, being careful to leave ⁵⁄₃₂ in (4 mm) at the thinnest point. The bangle is now at its most vulnerable as it is being held onto the lathe with the ⁵⁄₃₂-in (4-mm) wood, the depth of which can be hard to judge.

15 Sand the outside of the bangle with 600-grit wet-and-dry paper.

16 Attach the drill onto the right-hand side of the lathe, with the bangle on the left side. Wrap a cloth around the drill so that when you shear off the bangle, it will land on the drill wrapped in cloth rather than on the floor to soften the impact.

17 Shear off the bangle with a skew chisel.

18 Sand the inside of the bangle with a split pin and 240-grit wet-and-dry paper on the micromotor.

19 Seal with microcrystalline wax or the sealant of your choice.

10

13

11

17

14

18

16

12

19

Carving cork

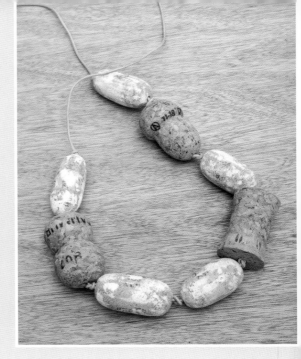

TOOLS AND MATERIALS

- Wine or champagne bottle corks
- Drill bits, ⁵⁄₆₄ in (2 mm) and ⅛ in (3 mm) sizes
- Drill press or micromotor
- Scalpel or craft knife
- Rough file
- Acrylic paint and paintbrush
- Wax varnish in a dead flat finish, or microcrystalline wax
- Sheet of 240-grit wet-and-dry paper
- Leather cord, ¹⁄₁₆ in (1.5 mm) in diameter

USING CORK BEADS

You can use this technique to adapt the Oak Broken Line Necklace (see pp. 109–113) by interspersing your wood squares with cork beads.

Many tree products can be used to make jewelry, including bark, roots, vegetable ivory, coconut shell, amber, and latex. Tagua- and ivory-nuts have traditionally been carved into buttons and can be dyed. I chose cork, the bark of the cork tree (*Querus suber*), because it can be sustainably harvested, with half the world's production coming from Portugal. It is available in carving blocks, sheet, cord, and bottle corks. Sometimes wine corks are made from natural cork, but more often they are made from reconstituted cork particles. Cork is so light that it is a good choice if you want to make something particularly large. For my example, I used wine and champagne corks, the latter being preferable because they aren't damaged by a corkscrew.

1 To make cork beads, mark your middle point at each end of the cork and use a ⁵⁄₆₄-in (2-mm) drill bit to drill into the middle from either end. To widen the hole in the cork, use a longer ⅛-in (3-mm) bit that will go all the way through.

2 Using a scalpel, cut away unwanted material from the cork to form your bead.

3 Refine the shape with a rough file.

4 Sand the cork bead smooth with 240-grit wet-and-dry paper.

5 If you want to color your beads, paint them with acrylic paint.

6 Seal the beads with wax varnish. Leave to dry.

7 Thread the beads onto leather cord, knotting in-between each bead. If you find leather hard to thread, try opening out the holes with the ⅛-in (3-mm) drill again, or just twisting the leather.

Shaping laminated veneers

TOOLS AND MATERIALS

- Piercing saw
- Piercing saw blade
- Wood block,
  5 x 3 x 1 in
  (120 x 80 x 25 mm)
- Scalpel
- Cutting mat
- Ruler
- Drafting tape
- Wood veneer, 3 strips
  ¹⁄₆₄ in thick x 1½ in
  wide (0.5 mm thick x
  30 mm wide)
- 2 C-clamps that can
  open up to 3 in (8 cm)
- Wood glue
- Glue spreader
- Pencil and paper

You can shape veneers into an interesting form by gluing and clamping together several layers in a jig until they dry. How many layers you need to combine will depend on what you are going to make with your finished shape, and, therefore, how strong the layer "sandwich" needs to be. The three ¹⁄₆₄-in (0.5-mm) layers I have used here would be strong enough to use for earrings, but you might need more layers to create a stronger result for other pieces such as necklaces or bracelets. The results of this process have a delicate quality, and you could experiment with differing wood combinations and constructions, perhaps riveting them together (see p. 94) or linking with jump rings.

1 Make a simple jig by sawing a curve in the block of wood.

2 Using the pencil, scalpel, cutting mat, and ruler, measure and cut your veneer into strips that are slightly wider than the width of your jig.

3 Layer your veneer with glue in between each layer. You can use masking tape to protect the jig from the glue.

4 Use the C-clamps to shape the veneer layers down into the jig; tighten the clamps. Leave to dry for the time recommended by the glue manufacturer.

5 Open up the C-clamps and then remove the curved veneer "sandwich."

6 Use the pencil and paper to make a template that will fit within the width of your wood "sandwich."

7 Tape the template onto the wood and saw out the shape.

8 Using the piercing saw, saw around the template to cut out the shape.

9 Sand the edges smooth and seal the piece with your preferred finish.

1

2

3

4

5

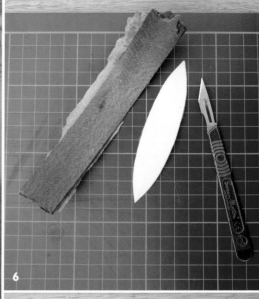

6

7

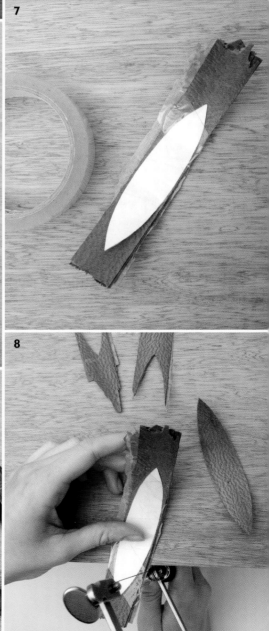

8

CHAPTER 4

Connecting

Making connections

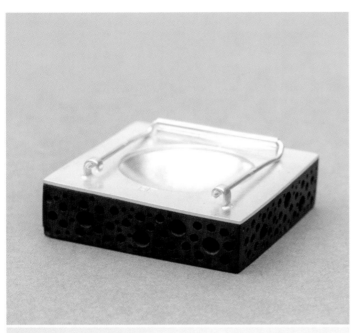

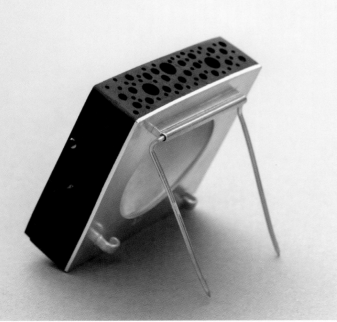

Cold connections (also known as mechanical connections) are key in allowing you to construct pieces of jewelry from materials that need to be joined together but would be damaged by the heat of a solder torch. This chapter introduces a range of options, but there are many variations you can create using these solutions. The projects in this chapter are designed to incorporate some of the most common and useful cold connections. Laser-welding is not covered in this book because access is limited to this expensive piece of equipment.

The simplest techniques use adhesives—cyanoacrylate or epoxy, applied with a pin—and plaque setting. This chapter also covers pinning either with silver wire (see the projects on pp. 26, 74, and 142) or with silver pegs soldered onto silver sheet used in the Bog Oak and Maple Striped Cuff Links (see p. 82). It also covers settings and rivets as in the plaque setting project (see p. 114); the claw setting on the Horse-Chestnut Burr Pin (see p. 96); wire rivets on the Ply Leaf Chain Riveted Necklace (see p. 88); tube rivets (see p. 94); and threading on the Oak Broken Line Necklace (see p. 108).

OPPOSITE AND LEFT Pierced ebony pin, right; set onto a silver sheet and showing the custom silver fastening, left.

Beech spoon necklace

This project is designed to show the versatile silver links that join elements together and articulate in all directions to make the piece sit well over the body. I wanted to use "found" objects, and since wooden spoons are made of hardwood and have an attractive shape, I found them to be an appealing option. I have seen jewelry pieces made from vintage rulers, colored pencils, golf tees, skateboards, spools, chess pieces, and handles. Some makers consider driftwood and green wood as found materials. Paints, inks, or other surface treatments (see p. 148) could be used, but I decided on the Japanese technique of *shou sugi ban* (also known as *yakisugi*) that is used to seal timber-clad housing by charring the wood. Easy to do, it is quite transformative, softening the edges of the wood and leaving a smooth surface. It doesn't leave sooty marks when finished, but I sealed the pieces anyway. The result is a very big statement, but you could alter the proportions using smaller spoons.

OPPOSITE Charred beech shapes made from wooden spoons and linked with custom findings in oxidized sillver.

TOOLS AND MATERIALS

- Piercing saw
- 4/0 metal saw blade
- Fine wood saw blade
- Pencil, paper, and scissors
- 13 beech wood spoons, 10 in (25.4 cm)
- Vernier caliper
- Rough file
- Micromotor
- Dust mask and goggles
- Solder torch and bricks
- Bench block or flat plate
- Reverse-action tweezers
- Wire brush
- 2 lengths of 1⅜-in (35-mm) square-section silver wire, with diameters of ³⁄₃₂ in (2.5 mm) and ⁵⁄₆₄ in (2 mm)
- Punches, ⅛ in (3 mm), ³⁄₁₆ in (4.5 mm), and ⁵⁄₁₆ in (9 mm) 10⅝-in (27-cm) square-section silver wire, ¹⁄₃₂ in (1 mm)
- Round-section silver wire, ¹⁄₃₂ x 4 in (1 mm x 55 cm)
- Fine file
- 240-grit and 1000-grit wet-and-dry paper
- Flat plate
- Hammer
- Polishing motor and mop
- Drill bit, ¹⁄₃₂ in (1 mm)
- Round-nose pliers
- Parallel-action pliers
- Paper towel
- Liquid detergent
- Cyanoacrylate glue
- Wax varnish, dead flat finish
- Silver oxidizing solution (platinol) plus safety equipment on solution label

1   Use the pencil, vernier caliper, and ruler to mark off 3¾ in (9.5 cm) on each spoon.

2   With the piercing saw, saw off the handles of the wooden spoons.

3   Use one of the spoons as a template to cut out paper pieces that can then be used to make a model.

4   The model is helpful when working out how many spoons you need, where to hang them, and how far apart they should be. You can hang it around your neck and adjust as necessary.

5   Use the rough file to shape the point and slope the underside into a nice shape.

6   Once the spoons are all shaped, use the vernier caliper and a pencil to mark ¾ in (20 mm) down from the top on each side.

7   Mark the middle of each side and then do the same on either side of the middle line, working with your vernier caliper set ⁵⁄₃₂ in (4 mm) apart.

8   Using the marks on either side of your central line, drill with the micromotor and ¹⁄₃₂-in (1-mm) bit to make two ¹⁄₃₂-in (1-mm) holes ⁵⁄₃₂ in (4 mm) apart and ¼ in (6 mm) deep. You can mark the drill bit with a pen to help judge the depth.

9   Now char the spoons using the solder torch and bricks, holding them with the reverse-action tweezers. You might need to blow out the flame if they catch on fire. Leave to cool.

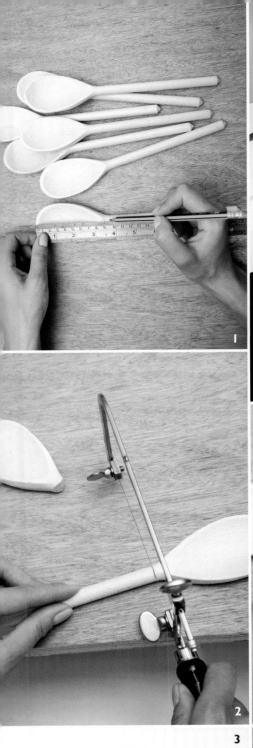

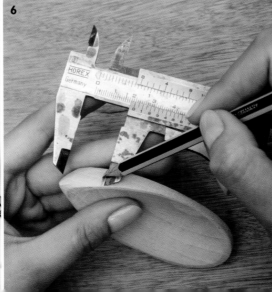

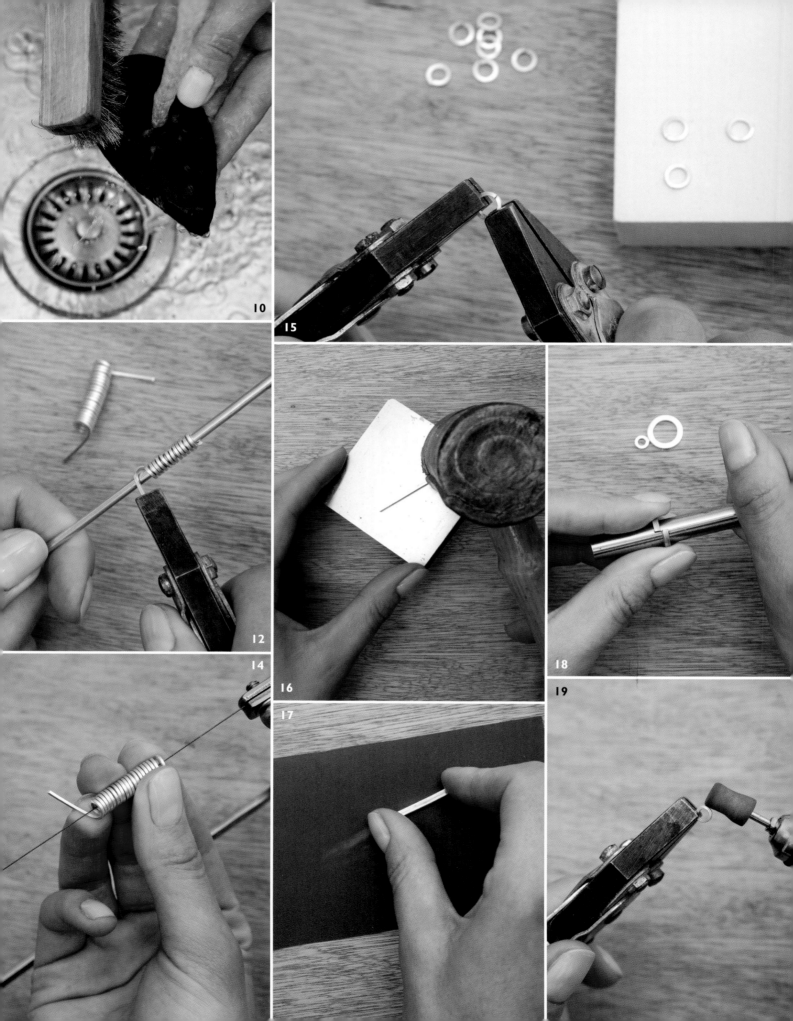

10 Remove any loose charring by running the spoons under the faucet and scrubbing with the wire brush.

11 Pat off the excess water with paper towels and leave to dry.

12 Now make the silver jump rings. For the 13 ³⁄₁₆-in (4.5-mm) rings, wrap the ¹⁄₃₂-in (1-mm) square wire around a ³⁄₁₆-in (4.5-mm) punch until you have made 13 round links.

13 For the five ³⁄₃₂-in (2.5-mm) rings, wrap the ¹⁄₃₂-in (1-mm) square silver wire around the ³⁄₃₂-in (2.5-mm) punch, until you have the required number of links.

14 To saw the rings apart, thread each spiral onto a piercing saw and cut through them with the method that was used for making ring findings shown in steps 10–13 on pp. 46–7.

15 Close the rings together carefully with two pairs of pliers. Place on the solder bricks when ready to be soldered closed.

16 To make the T-bar of the clasp, straighten the 1¼-in (35-mm) length of ³⁄₃₂-in (2.5-mm) square-section wire by tapping it with the rawhide mallet on all sides on the bench block or flat plate.

17 Put the 240-grit wet-and-dry paper flat on the bench and rub out any dents in the T-bar with sweeping strokes.

18 Make the round side of the clasp by wrapping the ⁵⁄₆₄-in (2-mm) square wire around a ⁵⁄₁₆-in (9-mm) punch or similar round object.

19 Clean up two of the ³⁄₃₂-in (2.5-mm) jump rings using a fine file and a polishing attachment on a micromotor or on a motor polisher if you have one.

20 Solder one jump ring onto the T-bar and one onto the large jump ring that will form the clasp using solder paste.

21 To finish the T-bar half of the clasp, attach a ³⁄₁₆-in (4.5-mm) jump ring onto the T-bar with three smaller jump rings and solder them closed.

22 Make the silver U-shapes to glue into the holes on your spoons by cutting 26 ¾-in (20-mm) lengths of ¹⁄₃₂-in (1-mm) round silver wire. Bend them into a U-shape using round-nose pliers.

23 Once all your silver parts are ready, wash them in boiling water and liquid detergent to remove any grease. Use platinol in a glass dish to oxidize these parts. It only takes a minute or two for the color to change. Then rinse and dry.

24 Rub these black findings with a silver cloth and leave to one side.

25 Paint the wooden parts with wax varnish. I used two coats underneath and one coat on the topsides.

26 Before gluing the silver links into the holes on the spoons, test the depth of the U-shape in the holes—about ⅛ in (3 mm) of the U-shape should be visible. Put cyanoacrylate glue onto a piece of plastic (as shown on the tip box on p. 122) and put three very small drops of glue down into the hole using a broken saw blade.

27 Using the parallel pliers, push the U-shape into the hole. You need to work carefully and push hard so that the U-shape doesn't get stuck halfway. You should not have excess glue coming out of the holes, but wipe it away immediately if you do. Repeat this process until all holes in the spoons are fitted with a U-shape.

28 Attach the clasp you made earlier using the same method, hooking the U-shape around the clasp and then gluing it into the holes.

Bog oak and maple striped cuff links

This project combines two useful techniques: laminating different woods together and attaching wood to silver sheet. Laminating woods is simple to do and full of possibilities. Silver sheet can be attached to wood using silver wire pegs; this is a versatile technique, but you need to make sure that the sheet is sitting tightly to the surface of the wood with no gaps. If you don't want to make cuff links, you could adapt this project to make stud earrings by replacing the cuff link findings with silver earring wire and butterfly earring backs.

OPPOSITE Two woods are laminated together to produce a striped pattern, highlighted by the beveled edges.

TOOLS AND MATERIALS

- Piercing saw
- Wood saw blades
- Metal saw blades
- Small C-clamps
- Belt sander
- 6¼-in (16-cm) half-round rough file
- Square angle
- 6¼-in (16-cm) half-round fine file
- Dividers
- Drill press or micromotor
- Small solder torch
- 2 solder bricks
- Acid bath
- Brass tongs
- Borax dish
- Small brush
- Riveting hammer
- Ball burr
- Flat plate
- 3 slices bog oak and maple, each ⅛-in (2.5–3 mm) (sold online for guitar heads)
- Wood glue and brush or plastic glue spreader
- Paint marker pen
- 2 pieces ¹⁄₃₂-in (0.8-mm)– thick silver sheet, approx 1 x ½ in (23 x 12 mm)
- Pair cuff link parts in silver
- Easy solder paste and/ or borax paste
- Acid for cleaning silver
- Epoxy glue or cyanoacrylate glue
- Wax or varnish finish

1 Using the piercing saw and a wood blade, cut five pieces of the two different woods, each 1 1/16 in (27 mm) wide and 4 1/16 in (103 mm) long. (This will make several pairs.)

2 Use a glue spreader to apply wood glue to each layer, making sure that the whole area is covered. The glue should not be too thick, as the woods need to touch; using too much glue can cause gaps.

3 Clamp the layers together using the C-clamps and leave to fully dry. Allow glue seep out at the sides if it wants to.

4 Remove the clamps from the wood layers and sand the sides and end of the layered piece with a file or a belt sander until they are completely smooth.

5 Using the square, mark out 9/32-in (7-mm) slices on the wood sandwich.

6 Saw off 9/32-in (7-mm) slices across the short end of the layered piece so you get a striped block of wood. Check that the end is straight with a set square as it needs to be accurately even.

7 Before you shape the wood parts further, make the silver parts. Using a piercing saw and a metal blade, cut two 1/2 x 1 in (12 x 23 mm) pieces from the silver sheet.

8 Place the silver sheet on solder bricks and solder the heatable half of the cuff link part onto the middle of the sheet, using easy solder and the solder torch. Use borax paste where you want the solder to flow. Repeat for the second cuff link.

9 Solder wire onto the other side of the sheet, balancing it between two solder bricks. Solder on two wires (I have soldered the wires 3/8 in [10 mm] apart) to each cuff link back.

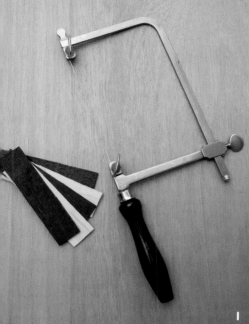

1

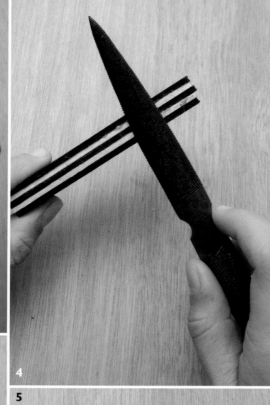

2

3

4

5

6

7

8

9

11

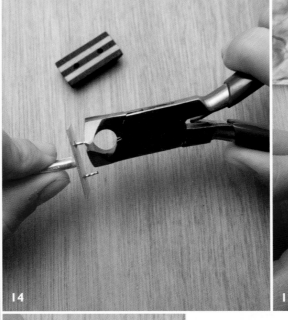

14

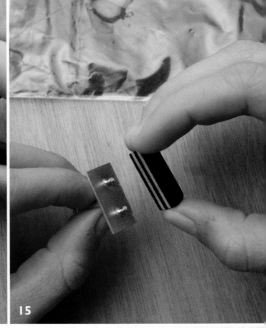

15

12

13

17

18

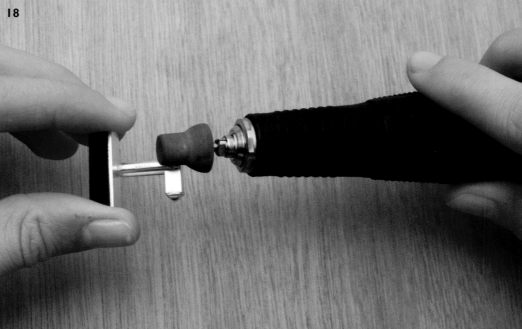

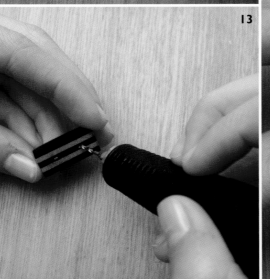

10 Using brass tongs, dip the soldered silver parts in an acid bath (see step 14 on p. 55).

11 File the striped wood slices so that they are marginally bigger than the silver sheet. File each side with the same slope at the edges. I have filed ⅛ in (3 mm) in at the top of each side. Using dividers set ⅛ in (3 mm) apart will help measure this. Use a rough file to remove material and then refine the shape with a fine file.

12 Mark where to drill into the holes in the bottom of the wood slices. Use the paint marker pen on the top of the wires and then transfer this to the back of the wood slice to mark the position.

13 Drill into the marked spots on the bottom of each wood slice to about halfway in.

14 Using end cutting pliers, trim your wires so that the wood fits down into the holes made in step 13, and that they are flush. If any solder around the bottom of the wire is preventing this, open out the hole slightly with a ball burr.

15 Glue the wood to the silver sheet.

16 Once the glue is completely set, file the silver sheet and wood back until it is completely flush with the wood and make any final adjustments with a fine file to make sure that the beveling is even on all sides.

17 Rivet the other half of the cuff link fittings onto the silver sheet using a riveting hammer on a flat plate. Tap each side to splay out the wire over the hole. Do this evenly, hammering both sides alternately until the rivet is secure and then tap with the flat side of the riveting hammer to flatten the surface.

18 Polish the silver fittings using a soft rubber burr on a micromotor. I have left these cuff links unsealed, but you could use varnish or wax on the wood.

TOOLS AND MATERIALS

- Pencil, cardstock, scalpel, and cutting mat
- Piercing saw
- 4/0 metal piercing saw blades (if cutting the ply by hand)
- Goggles and dust mask (if cutting plywood by hand)
- Plywood sheet, ⅛ in x 1¼ ft x 2 ft (3 x 400 x 600 mm)
- Steel wool
- Paintbrush
- Acrylic inks (I used ultramarine plus crimson for the accent links)
- Microcrystalline wax
- Micromotor
- Drill bit, ⅟₁₆ in (1.2 mm)
- Silver wire, ⅟₁₆ in (1.2 mm) in length
- End cutting pliers
- Rough file
- Flat plate
- Riveting hammer

Ply leaf chain riveted necklace

Riveting is a method for joining multiple repeat shapes created either using a piercing saw or through laser cutting. Contact your local laser-cutting service before you start to find out the type of laser-cuttable wood they supply, what CAD software you can send, and the size of their laser-cutting bed. The glues in some plywood make it unsuitable for laser cutting, and it makes sense to use wood your service can work with. You can also cut pieces out by hand using a piercing saw. If you wish to work manually, any ⅛-in (3-mm) birch plywood is fine. The rivets become a feature of the design, so think carefully about how they look. Because the links here are made up of different colors, this also makes a feature of the shape of each component part. A chain of this sort needs an even number of links. Make a model before you create the final piece to help you see how the chain will move and sit around the body.

OPPOSITE Painted and riveted laser-cut abstract shapes inspired by leaves form a striking chain necklace.

1 Experiment with cardstock, pencil, and a scalpel to make patterns and shapes.

2 Use the shapes you like as templates to create plywood models, cutting them out with a piercing saw. The edges of plywood fracture easily, and so it is better to use a fine metal saw blade to cut your models, rather than the coarser sort you would usually use for wood.

3 My design (see the drawing above) is 2 x 2½ in (50 x 65 mm) and overlapped to make links 2 in (50 mm) wide and 3$\frac{1}{32}$ in (93 mm) long.

4 Once you are happy with your design, make a CAD drawing with as many multiples as you can fit in the laser-cutting area of the machine that will cut them, and send your design to be cut. As an alternative, saw out the number of elements you will need by hand.

5 Paint your link shapes with acrylic ink and leave to dry with as little disturbance to the surface as possible.

6 Once dry, give the links a light sanding with steel wool to remove any raised wood grain and then paint with a second coat of ink.

7 Once the second coat is dry, add a layer of wax applied with a paper towel and leave to dry.

8 Place two link parts together in the way that you want them to look once they are joined. Hold them firmly while you drill a $\frac{1}{16}$-in (1.2-mm) hole through both pieces, making sure that your fingers are not in the path of the drill bit.

9 Thread a piece of $\frac{1}{16}$-in (1.2-mm) silver wire through so one side of the link is held in place.

10

11

12

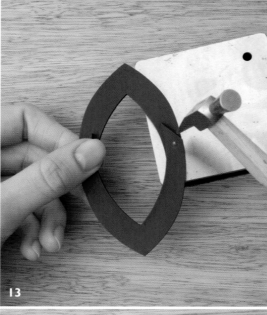

13

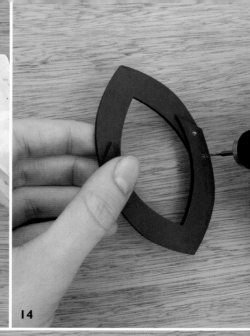

14

15

16

10 Swivel the two pieces so that they are held together in the right shape, then drill two holes on the other side of the link and thread the wire through both holes in the other side.

11 Using end cutting pliers, snip your two wires so that they are only sticking out ⅟₃₂ in (1 mm) either side of your wood links.

12 I find I can get a neater result at the next stage by filing the end of the wire flat before starting to hammer the wire.

13 Using the riveting hammer on a flat plate, hammer the end of the wire with the end of the hammer that has a ridge. You need to gently splay each end of the wire at the same time by alternating your piece from side to side. Once the ends have been splayed, hammer with the rounded end to finish.

14 Drill the other two lower holes in your first link and rivet (as in steps 10–13) so that the link is complete.

15 Place the first part of your next link through the first completed link, then close to connect both links to one another and repeat steps 8–14.

16 Repeat again until the whole piece has been constructed and is long enough to go over your head without a clasp.

Moving tube rivets

TOOLS AND MATERIALS

- Cardstock
- Micromotor
- Drill bit or ball burr, ³⁄₁₆ in (4.5 mm)
- 2 pieces of wood, ³⁄₁₆ in (5 mm) thick
- Silver tube, ³⁄₁₆ in (4.5 mm) outside diameter
- Punch, ¼ in (6 mm)
- Flat plate
- Hammer
- Piercing saw
- 4/0 metal saw blade
- Solder torch
- Solder bricks
- Acid bath
- Dust mask and goggles

You can use silver tubing to make flexible rivet connections that are similar to wire rivets by curving the edges of the tubing over the top of the wood around the holes. Wire rivets can also be made to move by using the same cardstock layering technique shown here. The flexible joint created by the tube rivet helps you to build chains similar to the Ply Leaf Chain Riveted Necklace shown on pp. 88–93.

1 Drill two ³⁄₁₆-in (4.5-mm) holes in your pieces of wood.

2 Start with small holes and then make them bigger if you are using a ³⁄₁₆-in (4.5-mm) ball burr rather than a drill bit.

3 Using the solder torch and solder bricks, anneal the tube to soften the silver.

4 Clean the silver tube in the acid bath.

5 Cut a length of silver tube that is approximately ⁵⁄₆₄ in (2 mm) longer than your two layers of wood plus the depth of the cardstock.

6 Thread the tube through the holes in the wood, leaving approximately ²⁄₃₂ in (1 mm) extra at the top and bottom. Place the piece of cardstock on either side, in between the two layers of wood.

7 Hammer either end of the tube using a doming punch, and alternating sides so that both ends are evenly curved.

8 Once the rivet is splayed out enough on either side to be secure, remove the cardstock. The two pieces of joined wood should be able to swivel.

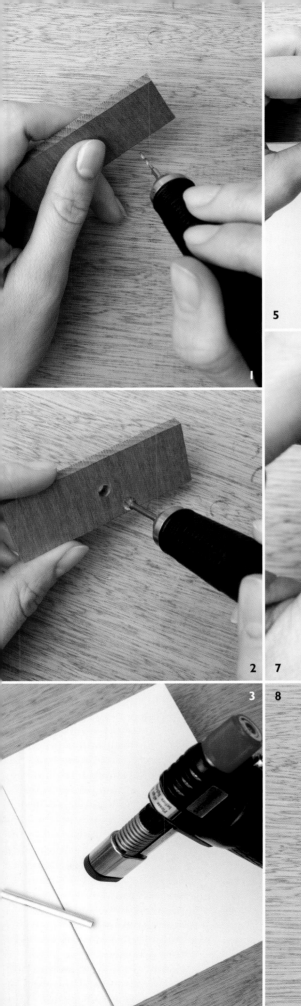

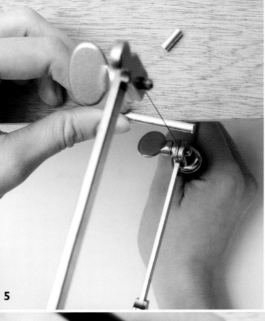

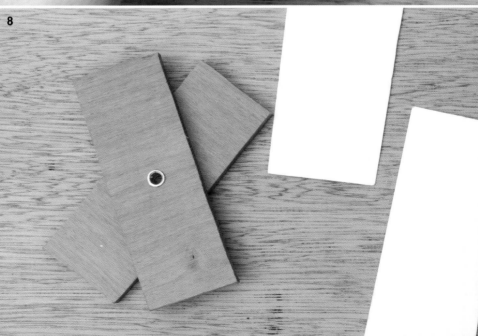

Horse-chestnut burr pin

This brooch project shows how you can use a claw setting to attach wood to a silver structure. I used a horse-chestnut burr since it had such an interesting, slightly surreal, surface. A burr is a sign of stress within a tree where it is under attack from fungus, virus, or injury. Makers prize burr wood for its creative possibilities and relative rarity. Pins are not the easiest jewelry finding to make, but you can adapt the principle to make a pendant by just making the main frame with the claws and omitting the pin back, then adding a jump ring at the top for hanging. The claw-setting technique shown here could be adapted for any piece of interesting wood, perhaps a piece of driftwood or a sandblasted, carved shape.

OPPOSITE A statement pin highlights the natural form of a horse-chestnut burr, set in a silver claw setting.

TOOLS AND MATERIALS

- Wood with bark
- Large, flat screwdriver
- Micromotor
- Wire brush mops
- Tracing paper, scissors, and pencil
- Half-round pliers
- Hammer
- Flat plate
- Rawhide mallet
- Solder torch
- Solder bricks
- Hard solder strip
- Rough file
- Fine file
- Square-section wire, 11 x $\frac{1}{16}$ in (390 x 1.5 mm)
- 2 lengths of $\frac{1}{32}$-in (1-mm) rectangular wire, 5 in (125 mm)
- 1½-in (41-mm) length of $\frac{3}{32}$-in (2.2-mm) silver tube
- Sheet of 240-grit wet-and-dry paper
- Binding wire
- Acid bath
- Parallel pliers
- Round-nose pliers
- Piercing saw
- Metal piercing-saw blade
- End cutting pliers
- Bleaching scouring powder
- Old toothbrush
- Microcrystalline wax

1 Lever the bark off the wood (see p. 12) using a strong screwdriver or something similar. You might need to saw down a suitable slice of the burr from a larger block using a band saw (see p. 162).

2 Clean off any remaining loose material using wire mops in a micromotor. Small ones are good for the job as they can get into the crevices of the wood.

3 Draw around the piece of wood on tracing paper. Use this to plan the shape of your silver frame by turning your paper over so it will match the back of your wood shape. My piece of wood measures approximately 4 x 5 in (10.5 x 12 cm).

4 Round off any sharp edges and finish the piece of wood as you want it to be in the final pin.

5 Scrub the wood with scouring powder. Rinse and leave to dry. Once dry, seal the wood with microcrystalline wax.

6 Using your outline drawing of the back of your wood piece, plan a simple shape for your frame and mark where there will be good places for your claws to be placed. I chose five places where they would sit happily, placed evenly around the pin. I have used 10½ in (27 cm) from the length of ¹⁄₁₆-in (1.5-mm) square-section wire.

7 Use half-round pliers (or round pliers if you don't have them) to bend the silver wire into the desired frame shape. If you are finding it hard to bend sufficiently, use the solder torch and solder bricks to anneal (soften) the silver, and then clean it in an acid bath to soften the wire.

8 Gently hammer the wire on a flat plate with a rawhide mallet.

9 With a solder torch—and placing the wire on solder bricks—use solder paste to solder the two ends of the wire together, closing the frame shape.

10 Clean up the seam with a fine file.

11 To make the brooch fixing supports, saw two lengths—I used 2¹¹⁄₆₄ in (55 mm) and 2⁹⁄₁₆ in (65 mm) here—of ¹⁄₁₆-in (1.5-mm) square wire. File them with a rough file until they are a nice fit in the frame. I used a 4¾-in (12-cm) length of square-section wire for my pin.

12 Hammer flat and then sand out any hammer marks before soldering the two lengths onto the frame.

13 Cut the wires for the claws from the rectangular wire so they will be long enough to bend around your piece of wood. Mine are between ½–¾ in (12–20 mm) long. File the ends flat so the pin is ready to solder.

14 Raise the frame on solder bricks to solder on the claws. Just heat the section of the frame near the claw you are going to solder.

15 Prepare the hooks for the pin fastening using two ¾-in (20-mm) lengths of ¹⁄₁₆-in (1.5-mm) square-section wire and cut a 1½-in (41-mm) length of ³⁄₃₂-in (2.2-mm) silver tube.

16 To solder on the pin fitting, turn your frame over, resting it on several solder bricks, allowing the claws to face downward.

17 Hold the silver tube in place with binding wire and the pin hooks with reverse-action tweezers and solder into place. Then clean up solder joints with wet-and-dry paper.

18 For the actual pin fastening, use hard-drawn wire, or if you have a draw plate, draw down ¹⁄₁₆-in (1.5-mm) round wire into ³⁄₆₄-in (1.2-mm) wire to harden it. Obviously, the pin fastening needs to stay nice and straight as you put the pin on and off.

19 Cut a longer piece of pin wire than you need and bend it into an L-shape. Thread one end through the tube and bend the other side with your hands. With the tube in place, you'll be able to obtain a sharp 45-degree angle.

20 Snip the ends of the pin to the right length with a pair of end cutting pliers and file into a point with a fine file.

21 To make some resistance on the pin fastening, use round pliers to kink the wire downward as close to the tube as possible.

22 Turn the piece over, position the wood into the finished pin and bend the claws over to hold it in place.

23 Use your hands to gently bend over the claws, and if the wood is moving, gently press down with pliers at the end.

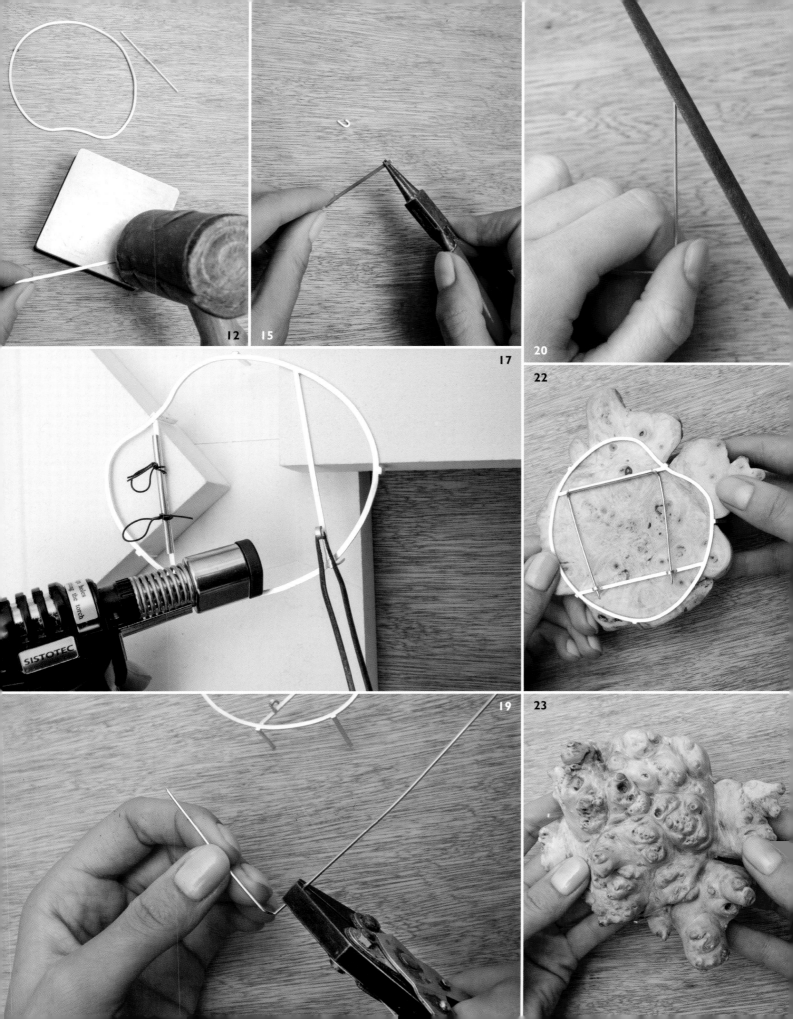

12

15

17

20

22

19

23

Stapling

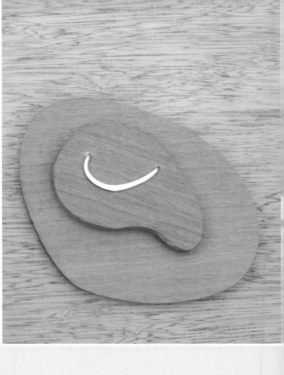

A method of joining two flat sheets of wood together, this stapling process would also work using acrylic sheet as one of the layers if you want to combine a wood sheet with a plastic. However, bear in mind that if you use translucent acrylic, the wires will show.

TOOLS AND MATERIALS

- Walnut sheet, chosen size, ³⁄₁₆-in (5-mm) thick
- Piercing saw
- 4/0 metal saw blade
- Fine file
- Rough file
- Silver wire, 1 ³⁄₄ x ³⁄₆₄ in (45 x 1.2 mm)
- Dust mask and goggles
- End cutting pliers
- Round-nose pliers
- Parallel pliers
- Flat plate
- Hammer
- Polishing bit
- Micromotor
- White paint
- Microcrystalline wax

1 Make templates of your chosen shapes from paper and cut out your two shapes from your walnut sheet using the piercing saw.

2 File around the sides of each wood shape with a rough file and soften the edge with a fine file.

3 Shape the silver wire with round-nose pliers.

4 Measure ¾ in (20 mm) from each end of the wire, and at this point, bend the ends of the wire 90 degrees using the parallel pliers.

5 If the ends are longer than ¾ in (20 mm), trim off the excess wire with end cutting pliers.

6 File the cut ends of the wire flat using a fine file.

7 Lay the curved top wire onto a flat plate and hammer flat.

8 Polish the top part of the silver staple using the micromotor and polishing bit.

9 Put a small amount of white paint on the end of the wires to help mark the wood so that the holes for your wires are drilled in the correct place and the right distance apart.

10 Drill a ³⁄₆₄-in (1.2-mm) hole through both sheets of wood, holding them very still so that both sets of holes are well aligned.

11 Thread the silver wire through the drilled holes in the wood—you should have about ³⁄₈ in (10 mm) sticking through—and bend it flat using your thumbs.

1

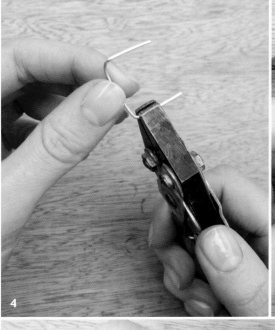

4

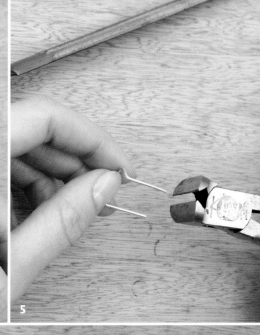

5

2

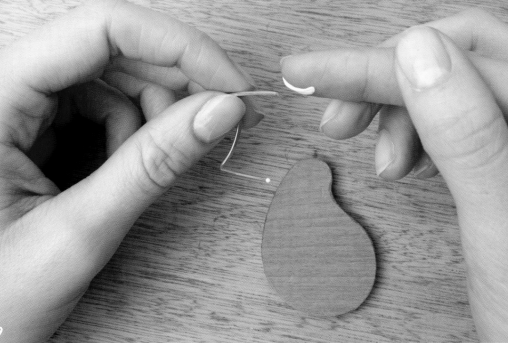

9

3

11

Terhi Tolvanen

Terhi trained as a silversmith at the Lahti Institute of Design, Finland, then attended the Gerrit Rietveld Academie in Amsterdam, Holland, where she learned reason working. Everything has a reason: the choice of the material, the shape, the logic of the piece; this underpins the themes that she gives to her work.

ABOVE Detail of *Source Chain* necklace in burned and varnished apple wood, synthetic spinl, and silver.

ABOVE *Adonis* necklace in painted grapewood linked and fastened with silver.

Are there artists or other influences that have been particularly important to your development?

Ruudt Peters, who was my teacher at the Rietveld Academie. It was from him I learned that everything must have a reason. "Follow your story and follow the qualities of your material," he would say, and "Don't think, just do." This approach helps my work, especially at the beginning of the process.

When I was still at school, the Czech sculptor and jeweler Pavel Opocensky came to give a lecture. I was very impressed by his way of working, where the rough stone saw marks were very visible on his pieces and at the same time the result was very fine and delicate. This is something I still admire a lot today, and my goal is to be rough but elegant in my pieces.
When I was doing my masters degree in Amsterdam, I had one (for me, crucial) conversation with my teacher Marjan Unger about the esthetic values of what I make. The question was for

whom do I make my pieces? [You] have to make a choice! For a long time, I shared a studio with Evert Nijland, whose passionate view of art and non-compromising vision about quality taught me so much. [This outlook has] been very precious to me ever since.

Can you describe your working process, such as your use of drawing, notebooks, and models?

I don't really draw. I sometimes make some little notes. I prefer working directly in the material. I start working by laying out my materials on a long shelf in my studio. The pins stay on the shelf but the necklace parts move quickly onto the mannequin, attached by tens of pins. Then I start putting things together, making parts, moving elements around the shelf and the mannequin while searching for good proportions and composition. Slowly the piece takes form and then final decisions can be made.

OPPOSITE TOP *Autumn Dots* necklace in
lavender wood, with paint and silver.

OPPOSITE BOTTOM Detail of
A Greenhouse for a Tree necklace in
painted hornbeam wood set with oyster
windowpane and silver.

*Do you source your own green wood and is there a lot of
preparation to make it stable for a piece of jewelry?*

I source my own green wood, mainly in the early spring. Garden
wood is not easy to find so I cut it on the side of little country
roads and in the forest. The wood needs to dry for at least three
to six months. When it is dry, I put it in the oven at 212°F (100°C)
to treat it against bugs.

*You have described the main theme of your work as the dialog
between man and nature. Could you tell us more about that?*

I'm fascinated by human interventions on nature: the need
to direct, control. Deciding how a tree is supposed to grow,
the need to have some nature around—for example, having
houseplants or making a garden out of a little balcony. But not all
is under human control; nature strikes back and grows moss or
rust on buildings, for example. There is a continuous interaction
between the two [and also] a lot of energy.

How do you balance ideas and functionality within your work?

I make my pieces to be wearable. I always make my necklaces on a mannequin. Even pins get a wearing check to check the weight and the best placement for the fastening. Functionality is part of the piece from the very beginning and often the original idea is adapted to the function. But the function can come from the idea too.

The linking mechanisms in your neckpieces look deceptively effortless. I imagine they are key in not distracting from the unity of a piece?

Yes, I have made a lot of branch pieces where I have reconstructed a branch in a shape I want it to be. In those cases, it is especially important that, visually, the piece makes one continuous piece of branch. This is also why I often choose a half-stiff construction.

Oak broken line necklace

This project explores making beads from standard hardwood dowel, available from a home improvement store. The stringing wire is fastened within a silver tube; this is strong and very versatile and can be adapted for any bead necklace. I've used oak, which has a strong grain. Woods without such a pronounced grain, for instance ash, might be easier to saw without splitting. There are so many designs possible using ordinary dowel rods (see the sidebar on p. 112), but for this particular design, you do need an accurate band saw.

TOOLS AND MATERIALS

- Band saw
- Mask and goggles
- Oak, ¾ x ¾ in (20 x 20 mm) and 3-ft (1-m) long
- Dividers
- Drill press or micromotor
- Drill bits, ⅟₁₆ in (1.5 mm) and ⅟₃₂ in (1 mm)
- Small paintbrush and dish for paint
- Varnish brush
- Piercing saw
- Wood saw blades
- End cutting pliers
- Small solder torch
- Solder bricks
- 240- and 1000-grit wet-and-dry paper
- Acrylic paint
- Wax finish varnish
- Ball burr
- 4 small round magnets
- 2-ft (60-cm) length of soft flex
- Solder paste
- 2 silver tubes, ⁵⁄₃₂ x ³⁄₁₆ in (4 x 5 mm) long
- Silver wire, ⅝ x ⅟₃₂ in (15 x 1 mm)
- Needle file
- 55 round wood spacer beads, ⁵⁄₃₂ in (4 mm)
- Crimping pliers
- Crimps
- Two-part epoxy glue

OPPOSITE Articulated square oak beads are punctuated with small round beads and defined by painted edges.

1 Saw 56 ³⁄₁₆-in (5-mm) slices from the oak on the band saw (see p. 162) to make 20 ³⁄₁₆-in (5-mm) square beads.

2 Put the 240-grit wet-and-dry paper flat on your bench and sand the sides and edges of each piece until smooth.

3 Mark the middle of each piece, using the dividers as a guide.

4 Set aside the two beads that will form the clasp. On the rest of the beads, drill a ¹⁄₁₆-in (1.5-mm) hole in the middle of each one using the drill press or micromotor.

5 Paint the edges of the square beads with acrylic paint.

6 Once they are dry, sand the sides on fine 1000-grit wet-and-dry paper to remove any excess paint.

7 Mark the position of the decorative line on the edge of each bead with dividers.

8 Make a shallow cut with the piercing saw to remove the paint. I made a line on the top half of the edge on two sides, a cut on the lower half of the side on one side, and left the fourth edge plain. This is to leave gaps in the lines as a design feature.

9 Seal the whole surface of the beads with two coats of wax varnish. Cover one half of each bead with varnish and leave standing on the unvarnished edge to dry. Turn over to do the other half. Repeat for the second coat.

10 To make the clasp, use dividers to measure a ⁵⁄₃₂-in (4-mm) length of ³⁄₁₆-in (5-mm) silver tube.

2

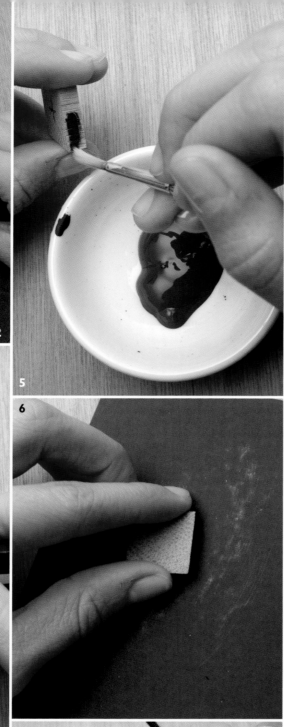

5

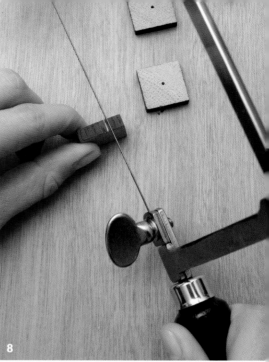

8

3

4

6

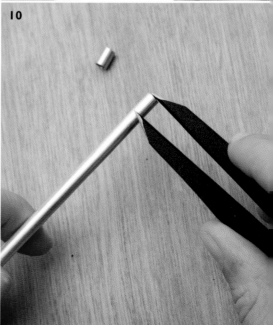

9

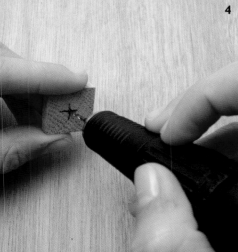

7

10

11 Drill a hole ⅛ in (3 mm) from the end of the measured length of tube.

12 Using a piercing saw, cut off the measured tube length.

13 Repeat steps 10–12 to mark, drill, and cut a second length of silver tube.

14 Using the solder torch and bricks, solder in a ³⁄₁₆-in (5-mm) length of wire with solder paste. The wire should stick out of the tube on either side (it will be filed flush at the next stage). It will be used to hold the soft-flex tube.

15 Using end cutting pliers, trim off excess wire then file down flush.

16 Mark the middle of the two wood bead squares you plan to use for the clasp and drill a ³⁄₁₆-in (4.5-mm) hole in each.

17 Glue in the cut lengths of silver tube. Leave to dry.

18 Mark the position for the magnets on both clasp squares. With a micromotor drill fitted with a ¹⁄₃₂-in (1-mm) bit, make an indentation deep enough for the magnets to sit flush with the wood. Start with the drill bit and then open it out with the ball burr.

19 Using a two-part epoxy glue, set the magnets down into the wood.

20 Thread the square beads onto the silver soft-flex wire, alternating with the round spacer beads. The size of the spacers will allow the square beads to bend around the neck without becoming too distracting from the overall design. At both ends of the wire, add two extra spacer beads.

21 To fit the clasp squares, thread the soft flex over the wire in the tube and crimp together to secure the wire. The crimp is secured to the soft flex in two stages. Crimping pliers have sections: use the section nearer the hands to squeeze the crimp into a U-shape, then use the further section to make the U round. Hide the crimp with small beads. Thread on all your beads and secure at the other end by crimping as before.

22 The finished clasp showing both halves of the magnetic closure.

alternative finishes

Experiment with different wood or dowel sizes and shapes to make a range of beads. Dowel rods are sold widely for various carpentry uses and are, therefore, available in a range of shapes, giving you endless scope for cutting and drilling it to make your own beads.

11

15

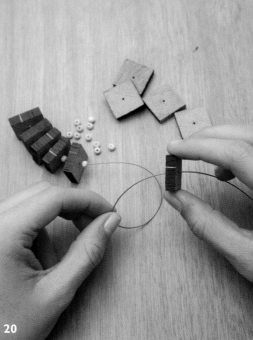

20

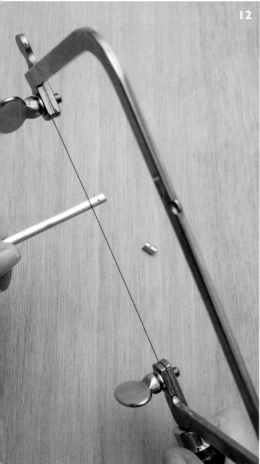

12

14

16

18

21

22

Plaque setting

TOOLS AND MATERIALS

- Piercing saw
- 4/0 metal saw blade
- Mask and goggles
- Silver sheet,
  $\frac{1}{32}$ x $1\frac{1}{4}$ x $1\frac{1}{2}$ in
  (0.8 x 30 x 37 mm)
- Carved wooden
  piece, 1 x $1\frac{1}{4}$ in
  (25 x 31 mm)
- Half-round pliers
- Silver strip for the
  collet, $\frac{1}{32}$ x $\frac{5}{32}$ x $3\frac{3}{4}$ in
  (0.8 x 4 x 95 mm)
- Silver strip for the
  loop, $\frac{1}{32}$ x $\frac{1}{8}$ x 1 in
  (0.8 x 3 x 25 mm)
- Solder
- Sheet of 240-grit
  wet-and-dry paper
- Rough file
- Solder torch
- Solder bricks
- Flux
- Round-nose pliers
- Two-part epoxy glue

Similar to bezel setting without the rub-over, a plaque setting is mainly used for setting flat-backed stones. However, you can also use it for other materials, including wood shapes. The collet (the metal frame that wraps around the edge of the item to be set) is lower than in a bezel setting, and the wood or object is glued in place. I made a silver loop for the setting to turn it into a pendant.

1 Use a piercing saw to cut out the plaque base from silver sheet, leaving approximately $\frac{1}{8}$ in (3 mm) of silver base around your item to be set.

2 Wrap a strip of paper around the wood shape to estimate the length of the strip of silver needed to form the collet.

3 Saw your silver strip slightly longer than you need.

4 Use half-round pliers to bend the silver strip to the shape of your piece.

5 Saw off the overlapping silver so it is exactly the right length to match the circumference of the wood shape.

6 Solder the strip ends together. This piece will become the collet to hold the piece.

7 Sand the bottom edge of your setting strip with wet-and-dry paper so that it sits flush on the base sheet.

8 Solder it in place from the outside, where it is easier to file off any excess solder.

9 File around the edge of the setting using a rough file.

10 Use the round-nose pliers to bend and shape the $\frac{1}{32}$-in (0.8-mm) silver strip that will become the loop.

11 Place the loop on solder bricks. With torch and flux, solder loop ends together.

12 Use the rounded side of the rough file to file the loop slightly so that the top edge of the egg-shaped setting sits into the curve of the loop.

13 Having sanded the top of the setting with wet-and-dry paper placed flat on the bench, hold it with reverse-action tweezers. Put facedown onto solder bricks, with the loop facedown and touching the setting. Prop the loop on a steel pin or solder probe to get it into the right position. Put solder on the joint and solder setting and loop together.

14 Clean up the solder joint and glue your wood piece (or stone) into the finished plaque setting.

CHAPTER 5

Surface Treatments

Decorating wood

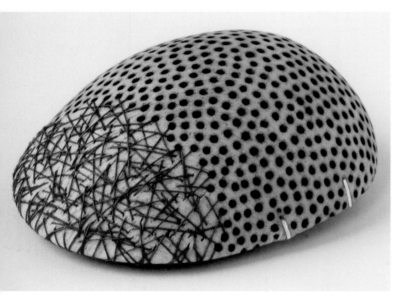

ABOVE Pin by Beppe Kessler, decorated with stitching and pyrography dots.

This Surface Treatments chapter takes a broad approach to the decoration of wood surfaces. The selection of material, construction, and finishing of wood jewelry all need to be considered in conjunction with one another. For example, the design of the Bog Oak Gold Spot Bangle on p. 132, with its indentations, was partly created to protect the gold gilding from being worn away. The surface gradually wearing away on a piece as it is worn, however, can be an interesting idea conceptually if it is a deliberate artistic intention.

There are two inlay methods shown that use silver wire to create dots or lines on the wood surface. Careful filing and sanding of the surface has given these inlays a smooth surface, so when selecting your wood, you will need to think about how any sanding and sealing of the wood might impact the silver. A real bonus of this technique is that no special equipment is required. The gilding technique needs some investment in tools, but has endless possibilities as a luxurious decoration to the wood below. Surface texturing is also explored with the use of sandblasting or, more simply, with different attachments to a micromotor. Electroforming actually coats natural objects in silver, and these can then be incorporated into jewelry pieces or become the central focus of a design. The color section and print transfer information are a reference source of suggestions, and will really come alive once you use them in a more fully shaped piece of wood or integrate them into a completed piece of jewelry.

OPPOSITE A selection of ebony rings decorated with inlaid silver lines (see p. 126).

Ebony silver dot pendant

TOOLS AND MATERIALS
- Ebony, approximately
  ³⁄₁₆ x 2 x 4 in
  (5 x 50 x 100 mm)
- Stencil (optional)
- Pencil or white crayon
- Dust mask and goggles
- Piercing saw
- Wood blades for
  piercing saw
- Ruler
- Paper
- Rough half-round
  metal file
- Hand drill
- Drill bit, ¹⁄₃₂ in (1 mm)
- Round silver wire,
  ¹⁄₃₂ x 4 in
  (1 x 100 mm)
- Small piece plastic
- Cyanoacrylate glue
- Sheet of 240-grit
  wet-and-dry paper
- End cutting pliers
- Round-nose pliers
- Baby oil and
  paper towel

A pendant is a good place to start working with wood because it requires no sizing or making of an identical pair. This design is realized using basic hand-sawing, drilling, and filling with pique decoration. The result is striking, despite the simple techniques involved. The elements that make this easy are the relatively thin ³⁄₁₆-in (5-mm) wood, the small ¹⁄₃₂-in (1-mm) dots, and their random pattern. I used a stencil for the overall shape. Draw your own design and think about how the decoration and hook relate to the overall form.

OPPOSITE Domed oval ebony pendant
with asymmetric silver detailing.

tip

To have firmer control over the glue coverage, put the glue onto a piece of plastic, dipping whatever you need to glue into it.

1 Use a pencil and a stencil to draw the outline of your pendant onto the wood. I used ebony, for a strong contrast with the silver dots.

2 Put on the dust mask—essential whenever you are doing work that produces dust. Holding your wood on the bench, start sawing the wood from wherever feels the most comfortable point. Cut slightly outside of your line, with long, loose strokes. Hold the saw vertical at all times or the top edge of the wood will be a different shape to the bottom edge. Make sure that your fingers are never in front of the saw blade.

3 Once you have sawed out the complete shape, use a rough half-round file to file out the saw marks from around the outside edge. Next, mark out the area of the highest point of your pendant using a pencil; this will act as a guide for you later when filling.

4 Using the flat side of your file, gradually file your wood into a gentle dome by leaving your highest point area untouched, and working further into the lowest points around the edge. Hold your piece up to eye level and check from the side view that the overall shape is even. Get the basic shape first, then refine the curvature with more gentle strokes.

5 Using the stencil, draw your design on a piece of paper until you are happy with how the area of dots will relate to the overall shape of the piece.

6 Cut out the shape of the area to be decorated from the paper.

7 Use the cut-out paper shape as a template to mark your design area on the wood.

8 Drill holes approximately ⅛ in (2–3 mm) deep, but don't go all the way through the wood. This is a random pattern, so I have not marked the wood beforehand, but you can do that in pencil first if you prefer. You also need to make one hole of the same size at the top of your piece, on the narrow edge, to glue in a hook on which to hang the pendant.

9 Once all your holes are drilled, put some glue on a piece of plastic and get a length of 1⁄32-in (1-mm) round silver wire.

10

13

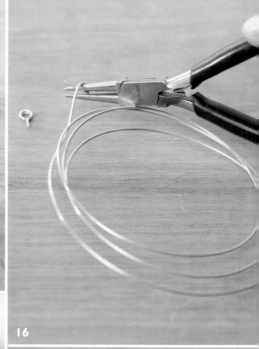

16

11

12

15

17

18

10 Dip the end of the wire into the glue and push it down into the first hole. If you are finding it hard to get the wire into the hole, it can help to hold the wire in some pliers low down, near to the wood.

11 Using end cutting pliers, clip off the excess wire as close to the wood as possible. Don't worry if some glue is showing on the pendant as it can be removed later.

12 Work your way across the area to be decorated, repeating steps 10 and 11 until all the holes have been filled with silver wire.

13 Now using the rounded side of your rough file, file gently over the exposed top of the wires. Keep going until they are completely flush with the wood.

14 Next, wrap a piece of 240-grit wet-and-dry paper around the file and continue to file. A good way to know when to stop is to close your eyes and run your thumb over the pendant. If it feels completely smooth, you're done.

15 Lay a sheet of 240-grit wet-and-dry paper flat on your bench. Place the pendant on top and rub it around in circular movements to flatten the back of the piece.

16 Wrap some of the silver wire around the round-nose pliers to form a simple hook, and cut it off at the right length for your pre-drilled hole.

17 Once you have checked the length in the hole, glue the hook into the hole by dipping the straight end in the glue as in step 10.

18 Wipe the surface with baby oil on a paper towel to bring out the luster of the wood and create the maximum contrast between the wood and the silver detailing.

alternative finishes

The variations on the pique technique are endless. There are many different wire clusters patterns you can create, as well as a wide range of silver wire thicknesses to try. Any change in silver wire dimension must obviously have the corresponding size hole.

You could use different wire and tubing to create a representative shape such as a flower. The inlay is done in exactly the same manner as the dots, except that the tube needs to be sawn off with the piercing saw.

Silver inlay lines

TOOLS AND MATERIALS

- Pencil and scalpel
- White marker or chinagraph marker
- Drill press or micromotor
- Ball burr, ⅟₁₆ in (1.5 mm)
- 6¼-in (16-cm) half-round rough file
- Fine file
- End cutting pliers
- Parallel pliers or a flat plate and mallet
- Cardstock for template
- Silver wire (design determines length), ⅟₁₆ in (1.5 mm) thick
- Cyanoacrylate glue
- Sheet of 240-grit wet-and-dry paper
- Wood of choice
- Dust mask

Using inlaid lines

You can use this technique to adapt several of the projects in this book:

- Ebony Silver Dot Pendant (see pp. 120–5): inlay silver lines rather than dots on your pendant.
- Bog Oak Gold Spot Bangle (see pp. 132–7): replace the indentations with inlaid lines in gold or silver wire.

You can use this technique to decorate any flat piece of wood. For some ideas of how to incorporate it into other projects in the book, see the panel below left and the image on p. 119. Use it as a starting point for your own designs, too.

1 Make a template for your design using cardstock and a scalpel.

2 Mark the position of the inlay on the wood using your template and white marker. It is easier to do this inlay on a flat surface if you're trying it for the first time.

3 Use the ⅟₁₆-in (1.5-mm) ball burr held like a pencil to lightly mark a guideline on the wood. Starting very gently, hollow out the channel until it is deep enough for the wire to go down into it and sit half-in and half-out of the wood.

4 Using end cutting pliers, cut your silver wire to the correct length.

5 File the ends flat, using the half-round rough file.

6 Tap the wires with the mallet until they are flat without distorting the shape of the wire.

7 When you are happy with the fit of the silver wire in the channel, flood the channel with cyanoacrylate glue and sink the wire down into it. Don't worry if the glue looks messy around the sides of the wire. Leave the glue to set completely.

8 Starting gently and using the fine file, file across the silver line until it is flush with the wood surface. If you close your eyes and sweep your fingers across the wire, you should not be able to feel it.

9 You can fill any gaps between the wood and the wire with a little glue mixed with sawdust from the same wood. Allow the piece to dry before filing again.

10 Put the wet-and-dry paper flat on table and sweep the piece across it until the surface is completely smooth.

1

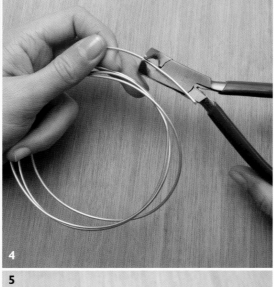

4

5

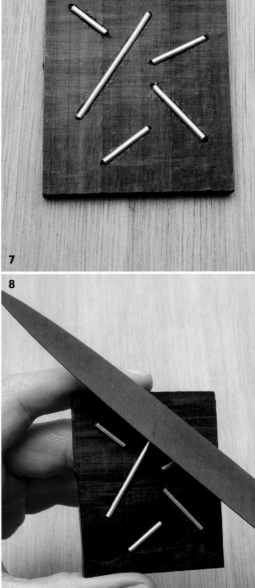

7

8

2

3

6

10

Beppe Kessler

Beppe trained at the textile department of the Gerrit Rietveld Academie in Amsterdam, Holland in the late 70s. After spending time as an industrial textile designer, she went on to work as a jeweler and painter.

What are the main themes of your work?

I always have been interested in themes that you can't easily grasp: huge concepts like time, space, weather, nothing. My work has to tell a story that is clear to myself. In 2008, I made a collection about carrying time with you in a pin, called Ocean of Time, with pieces like *What Time Is It, It Is Late, Slowly, Long Time,* and *Now and Then.* Later, I worked with the concept of space, to create landscape-like pins, realizing that having a home or having space or room around you is one of the most precious things there is. At the moment, I am fascinated by the theme of nothing. It is a challenge carrying "nothing" with you in a pin. Maybe things that are no-thing hold everything inside.

What was it about jewelry that you felt opened up more artistic possibilities, replacing your earlier work in textiles?

Textiles were the perfect choice for me, as I liked the idea of working with a diversity of materials. Not only sensitivity, but also for color, for structures, for repetition. And my focus has always been to push materials to their limits and look at how to combine them in new ways in any medium I work with. When I worked as a textile designer, I liked seeing my drawings and paintings transformed into high-quality printed fabrics, but although I was proud of these textiles, the job didn't give me enough artistic freedom. The turning point came when I was commissioned to create a unique carpet for a government building in the Hague. This gave me more freedom than my previous work. I realized that my heart was in working autonomously with jewelry and painting, and combining the two, so that is the path I went on to pursue.

OPPOSITE TOP *La Condition Humaine* necklace features balsa-wood carved beads interspersed with small coral beads.

LEFT *Over and Over Again and Always* pin, crafted in balsa wood and brass.

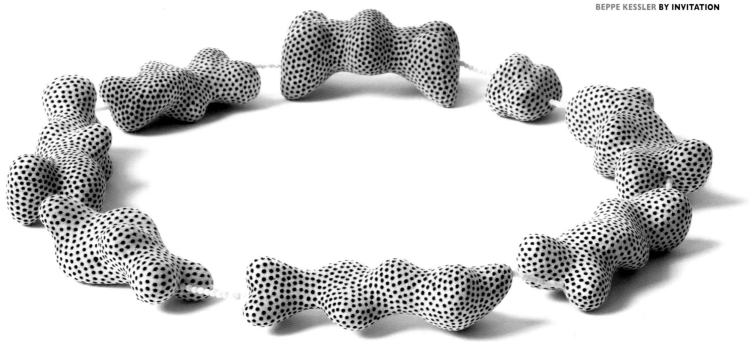

Are there artists or other influences that have been particularly important to your development?

Eva Hesse was important in the beginning. Robert Ryman, the Zero movement (Jan Schoonhoven), and Sheila Hicks. I admire Giuseppe Penone. I recognized their way of working; it was a confirmation of my own path and inspiration as well.

Can you describe your working process, your use of drawing, notebooks, models, etc.?

Thinking is always the first step. And I have to feel an urge to make something. In the beginning, there is a vague knowledge of where it is heading. Sometimes, a word is the starting point: time, space, nothingness. Sometimes a question: will it be possible to... Questions to me are more important than answers.

With jewelry, I start to work with material and make material sketches: numerous samples of unfinished packed, sculpted, or glued materials. I think with my hands. In fact, there is an intelligence in the hands that is different from that in the brain. I have to carefully watch what happens in my hands and stop at the right moment. Mistakes are more interesting than perfection; they can lead you to an unexpected path.
My material comes from everywhere: all kinds of wood, coal, alabaster, bone, pieces of rough materials, [all] found discarded, scattered around, in nature or in my everyday environment, soft

enough to form by means of a power file. I always work from big to small; that means I start with a big chunk of material and slowly reduce its form. I push materials to their limits and even further until they break. The way a material breaks shows its vulnerability. That is an interesting point, its true identity.

Wood is one of my favorite materials to work with. It is rather easy and patient, with an enormous variety of types, each with different qualities. It is a living material, growing in circles, in year rings. You can read time from it. You can give it so many faces: leave it rough, or make it soft and glancing. Burn it, cut it drill it, break it, bend it, and even embroider it.

I like to combine weak and strong materials, like soft balsa wood and metal, together. If you form them with the same effort, the soft material sculpts more easily than the strong material and that is interesting (see the pin *Over and Over Again and Always*, opposite). You can play with that, make use of that fact, and develop a method to handle the two together.

Do your painting and jewelry inform one another?

Sure they do. When I am painting, I get ideas for jewelry and vice versa. Since the very beginning of my career, I have made both and I never made a choice between being a painter or a jeweler; I am both. It is a choice not to choose. Painting on aluminum inspired me to use this technique on a smaller scale in a pin.

Embroidering the linen in a painting brought me to embroidery on balsa wood in jewelry. I worked for a few years using embroidery on balsa wood and developed a kind of language in that. But I also translated this process again to bigger objects with burnt balsa to hang on the wall, similar to paintings. So, in summary, there is always an interaction. It is an ongoing story, working in two fields at the same time.

You have described yourself as being a hands-on materials person—could you talk about your material experimentation?

Jewelry you hold in your hand, watching closely. You start with something, a volume. Intellectually, you can think a lot and invent concepts, but, after all, the physical thing has to convince and communicate the story. By immediately starting to work with material—sometimes led by intuition—you follow another path, parallel to a vague intellectual direction. Thoughts are a motor; they do not wait. They ask for a touching of material, making lots of samples in trial and error. What comes out looks like chaos, without a straightforward direction, but it generates possibilities and impossibilities you did not think of before,

charms or unexpected directions. And other words emerge. There always is a cooperation and intelligence between the hands and the eye, with critical thoughts in between. Words are limited. I am not a poet, but I like to make poems through materials, which tell a story.

I was interested that you have avoided learning traditional jewelry techniques, such as soldering, in order to find your own solutions. Could you describe the tools and techniques that you have developed?

In a way, it is a freedom not to be educated as a jeweler (nor a painter), although it sometimes costs a lot of extra time, but it also leads me to other ways. When you haven't learned certain skills, there are no rules except for your own. Because I have no jewelry skills, I have to solve problems differently. Over the years, I started to get a feeling for how to handle metal and gold in my own way, without soldering. If I could master soldering, an overwhelming quantity of possibilities would emerge. However, until now I haven't felt the urge to learn it. And moreover there are enough colleagues who master it, so why should I?

LEFT *Eyebright* pin in balsa wood, brass, and bone.

Limitation is also my strength. And the way that my work will develop is probably freer and more unpredictable as a result.

In the beginning, I used gold leaf rather as a color, a surface on top of another material. I now use plate material, as a sheet. And with a hand sawing machine and epoxy, I glue the metal into the wood in such a way that it becomes a part of the image. That is all I need. So there are not many tools that are necessary. Sometimes students are surprised that I use only a few machines and don't master many skills and still it looks professional. . . .

How do you balance ideas and functionality within your work?

That is always a struggle. Some ideas are the strongest at the sketch stage and lose strength as soon as you try to transform them into jewelry, so they are waiting for a solution. It is a challenge to find a way. In my paintings, I am totally free, but in the jewelry, I really want to make the pieces wearable without losing any quality. It is possible, I know, and I do not go for less. In a pin, it is easier than in a necklace; it can be an object as well, and the closure can be an integrated part of the object, as for example in the pin *Over and Over Again and Always* (see p. 128).

It takes time to develop ideas without thinking of the end result. In the end, there is always a limitation because you have to think within the possibilities of functionality. But that also forces you to be inventive and free yourself from these limitations.

ABOVE Embroidery and beading is used to decorate this wood pin.

ABOVE *Encounters* pin in yarn-wrapped wood, vinyl, acrylic, resin, and lava.

TOOLS AND MATERIALS

- Scalpel and cutting mat
- Small paintbrush for glue
- Bowl
- Skillet
- Rabbit skin glue
- Bog oak, ⅜ x 4 x 3¾ in (10 x 100 x 95 mm)
- Micromotor or handheld drill
- Dust mask and goggles
- Belt sander
- Piercing saw
- Wood and silver piercing saw blades
- 6-in (15-cm) half-round 00-cut rough file
- 6-in (15-cm) half-round 4-cut fine file
- Dividers
- White multi-surface paint pen or chinagraph marker
- Ball burr, ¼ in (6 mm)
- Palette knife
- Gilder's tip (soft brush for gilding)
- Gilder's pad
- Gilder's knife
- Round-tipped agate burnisher
- Pencil and cardstock
- 240- and 1000-grit wet-and-dry paper
- Gold leaf
- Petroleum jelly
- Cotton balls
- Cotton swabs

Bog oak gold spot bangle

The design of this dark wood bangle uses texture to protect the gold leaf in small indentations, creating a dramatic contrasting pattern. The technique is an adaptation of water gilding, done directly onto the wood without the usual gesso or bole foundation layer underneath. I have used a red-gold shade, but there are many different hues available in metallic leaf.

OPPOSITE Bog oak bangle decorated with carved, gilded indentations.

1 If you want to make this piece in one day, you will need to soak the rabbit skin glue granules overnight in a bowl with eight parts water to one part granules.

2 Draw your inside bangle edge on a sheet of cardstock with a pencil. I have drawn around a 3 x 2½-in (75 x 64-mm) oval silver bracelet. You can test the size by cutting it out of the cardstock and seeing how it fits over your hand.

3 Draw around your cardstock template onto the bog oak.

4 Drill a ¹⁄₁₆-in (1.5-mm) hole in the negative space (what will be the empty area) near the edge of your interior oval shape using a micromotor or handheld drill.

5 Thread your piercing saw blade through the hole and tighten the blade by compressing the frame. Saw out the inside shape, being sure to keep the saw vertical.

6 File the inside edge smooth using a rough and then a smooth file.

7 Open your dividers to the same width as the wood and use the inside edge to mark your outside edge. It might help to make the line clearer with the white paint marker pen.

8 Saw along your outside edge and file smooth using the fine file.

9 Using a belt sander or a rough file, start to shape your bangle, working on the inside edge first.

2

3

4

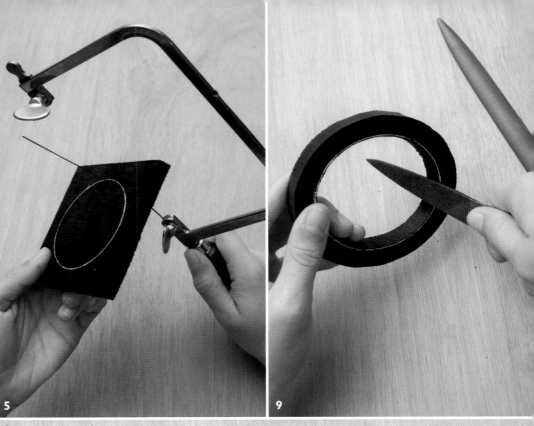

5

9

8

10

13

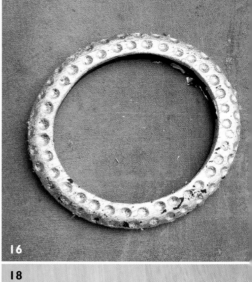

16

11

14

18

12

15

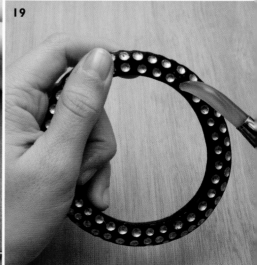

19

10 This design leaves the inside edge straight but domes the outside edge. When you are happy with the shaping of your bangle, use the ¼-in (6-mm) ball burr to drill your cup-shaped indentations. Practice on a scrap piece of wood until you feel confident to work on your finished piece. The gilding works best if the cup shapes are smooth.

11 Put the bowl of rabbit skin glue into a saucepan of freshly boiled water and stir until the granules dissolve. Do NOT boil the glue as it will lose its ability to stick. Once dissolved, paint the glue onto the area of the bangle that you want to gild and let it soak in.

12 Put petroleum jelly on the back of your hand, then brush the gilder's tip over it several times. This will make it easier to pick up the gold leaf.

13 Place the gold leaf on the gilder's pad and use the palette knife to cut the sheet of gold leaf into manageable slices.

14 Lift the gold leaf onto the bangle with the gilder's tip.

15 Use cotton balls and an up-and-down dabbing motion to ease the gold leaf into the indentations on the bangle.

16 Cover the whole glue-brushed area with gold leaf. Some areas might need a second or even third layer, so reapply glue as before and fill in any gaps.

17 Leave to dry completely for 3–6 hours.

18 Using wet-and-dry paper, sand the flat areas back, leaving the indented gold detail unsanded.

19 Burnish the wood surface all over with the round tip of the agate burnisher for a shiny finish.

alternative finishes

A range of different gold leaf decoration on bog oak, right. Experiment with creating textures on any hardwood using burrs, engraving tools, etc., to create different patterns for gilding within.

On the far-left sample, no tool was used; just the wood grain on the bog oak itself was treated with gold leaf, resulting in an interesting effect. Gold leaf comes in many different metallic colors, so you will be able to create plenty of variations by working on a range of woods.

Lina Peterson

Swedish-born Lina Peterson graduated from the
Royal College of Art with an MA in Goldsmithing,
Silversmithing, Metalwork, and Jewelry. She currently
lives and works in London, England. Her work has been
featured in exhibitions around the world, and is held in
public collections in the UK and Sweden.

ABOVE Detail of a pin from the Carved in
Color collection.

Can you describe your working process, your use of drawing, notebooks, 3D models, etc.? Do these differ with any other strands of work?

Often, a new piece of work comes directly from a technical discovery, making an earlier piece, something stumbled upon, or the way something might look before it was completed—that was interesting enough in its own right—to be explored further. I do draw, I sketch quick ideas, and I like looking back at these to see how my thinking develops, or more often than not, revisits the same ground in a different way. Testing forms a big part of how the work develops, to such an extent that it is becoming more and more part of the actual practice of making.

Are there artists or other influences that have been particularly important to your development?

I admire jewelers and artists who do something interesting with materials, something that feels intuitive but is in fact the result of great knowledge and understanding of materials. I love the work of Karla Black, Phyllida Barlow, Iris Eichenberg, Richard Tuttle, and Sally Marsland. To me, their work is brave, innovative, and sometimes [even] reckless.

You have always used a wide range of materials but wood seems to be increasingly central—what is the reason for that? Is there a particular role that wood plays in juxtaposition with other materials?

For me, working with wood is closely linked to working with color and, in many ways, that is what's driving the work. Working with wood doesn't actually come naturally to me, but, perhaps in

BELOW Necklace from the Carved in Color collection.

ABOVE *Yellowly* pin; Exploring Color series commissioned by the UK Craft Council.

LEFT *Flora* necklace, petal forms with abstract patterns inspired by flower colors. In limewood, resin, and glitter-set resin.

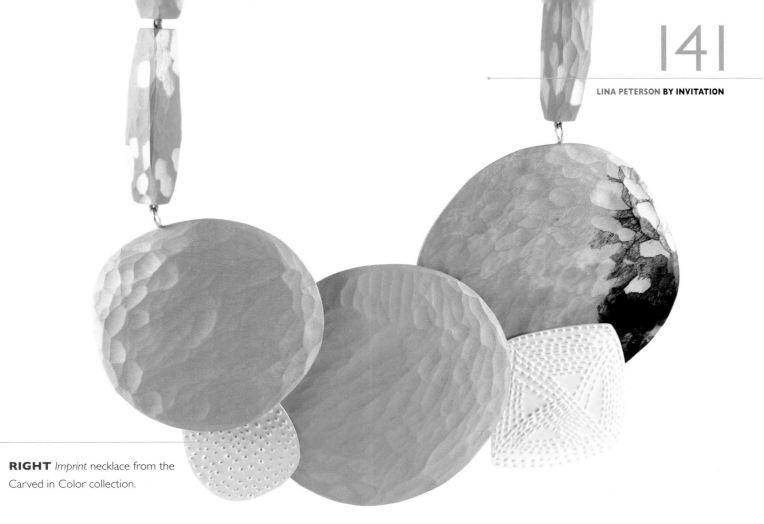

RIGHT *Imprint* necklace from the Carved in Color collection.

that challenge, there are also possibilities. The fact that there can be a friction there, a frustration with the material, is perhaps why I haven't got bored of working with it.

I began to work more with wood because it takes color very well and it's reasonably durable. For these reasons, I work almost exclusively with limewood, as it is very pale and easy to carve. I do keep working with a range of materials, though, but sometimes one dominates over the others.

Can you talk about the different techniques you have used to incorporate wood into your pieces—riveting, casting, carving?

For much of the work, such as the Carved in Color series, see the pieces shown above and left top and bottom, carving plays a central role. In these pieces, carving becomes the technique that creates form, but it is also a tool that creates a tension between surface and material, between color and the wood itself. In earlier work where I combined a range of materials in one piece, I made use of rivets. I often use concealed pins that are soldered onto metal and glued in place within the wood.

What are the central themes in your work? And are there subjects that you find yourself returning to?

My work consists of specific material explorations into wood, textiles, plastics, and metal. Working with how color and material come together to create a visual dialog about process, form, and surface is at the core. Sometimes this can be quite gestural, sometimes bold.
The use of color has always been central to my work, and this is something I'm now beginning to look at more deliberately through my research.

How do you balance ideas and functionality within your work?

Originally, this is what drew me to jewelry—the possibility of materiality combined with the constraints of wearability. Now I'm not so sure!

Often my work is big, but not all of the time. Everything I make is wearable and the body is considered, but at the core of my work is always the idea.

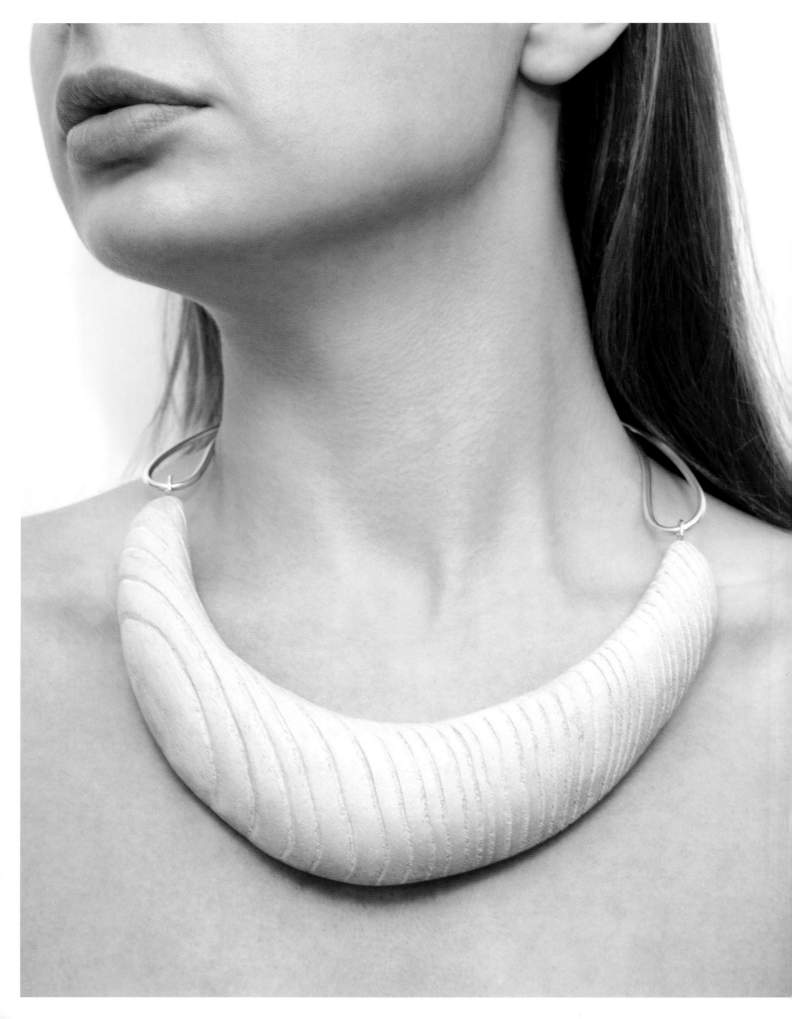

Oak strata necklace

The shaped wood part of this necklace has been professionally sandblasted to accentuate the wood's grain. Sandblasting equipment will propel sand or another abrasive material against your chosen surface under intense pressure inside a special chamber in order to smooth or roughen the surface. The process works better on woods that have differing density of wood from winter and summer growth. I have shown two finish options: waxed oak with silver findings and ebonized oak with oxidized silver findings.

OPPOSITE Silver and sandblasted oak version of the strata necklace.

TOOLS AND MATERIALS

- Paper and pencil
- Scissors
- Band saw or piercing saw with wood saw blade
- Belt sander
- Micromotor
- Rough file
- Dust mask and goggles
- 3 round objects, ⅜ in (10 mm), ¼ in (6 mm), and ⁵⁄₆₄ in (2 mm) in diameter
- Half-round pliers
- Solder torch
- Solder bricks
- Vernier caliper
- 2 pairs parallel pliers
- Acid bath
- Rubber polishing mops
- Fine steel wool
- Silver cloth
- Drill, ¹⁄₁₆ in (1.5 mm)
- Silver oxidizing solution
- Flat-based pyrex dish, at least 5 in (12 cm) long
- Brush
- Oak, 1 x 7 x 6 in (2.5 x 18 x 15 cm)
- 4-in (10-cm) length of ³⁄₃₂-in (2.5-mm) round silver wire
- 4-in (10-cm) length of ³⁄₆₄-in (1.2-mm) round silver wire
- 4-in (10-cm) length of ¹⁄₃₂-in (0.8-mm) round silver wire
- Easy solder paste
- Easy solder strip
- Ebonizing solution (see pp. 152–3)
- Microcrystalline wax
- Two-part epoxy glue

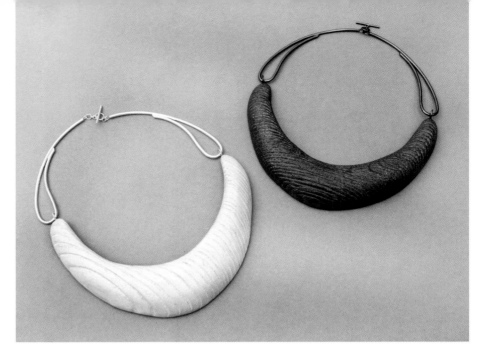

1 Cut a paper template of your necklace shape, folding it in the middle to make sure that it is symmetrical. Hold it up against your neck to check that you are happy with the shape and proportions on the body.

2 Saw the outline shape from wood with a band saw (see p. 162). If you don't have access to a band saw, you can use a piercing saw, but with this depth and a dense wood like oak it will be slow work.

3 Round the inside curve with the rounded end of the belt sander and then sand the whole piece to the desired shape. Refine any ridges and shape with a rough file.

4 Get the cut wood sandblasted. In the step 4 photo opposite, the left piece is before sandblasting, and the right is after.

5 These test pieces show the effect of sandblasting on different woods. Top to bottom step 5 photo opposite: oak, cedar, ash, sequoia.

6 Make a guide drawing for the shape of the main silver parts of your necklace. I estimated an approximate size by noticing that the wood went halfway around the neck, so I knew I needed something of a similar size again.

7 Saw two 8½-in (22-cm) lengths of ³⁄₃₂-in (2.5-mm) round silver wire and anneal them using a solder torch and bricks so that they are easier to shape.

8 With your drawing as a guide, use the curve of your wire and gently manipulate the first length of wire with your hands or bend it around a similar curved object. Half-round pliers can also be useful to carefully adjust the curve without marking the silver.

9 Once the main curve is right, curve the bottom end around a ⅜-in (10-mm) diameter object until it is almost parallel to the first curve. Use your thumb or a curved shape to curve inward until the top meets your first curve.

10 Saw the bottom part of the wire at a sloping angle with a piercing saw. File the sloping end flat and round the edges.

11 Repeat steps 7–10 with the wire curving in the opposite direction to make the second silver necklace part.

12 Using the solder torch and bricks, solder the sloping ends of both silver parts to the main curves with easy solder or solder paste.

13 Next, prepare all the pieces for the clasp and the wood attachment. Start by winding ³⁄₆₄-in (1.2-mm) round wire around a ¼-in (6-mm) object, forming a coil.

14 Then saw off three jump rings from your wire coil. If you need guidance, see the information about making jump rings on pp. 46–7.

15 Wrap ¹⁄₃₂-in (0.8-mm) wire around a ⅛-in (3-mm) object (I used the handle of a needle file) and saw off four rings.

16 Wrap ¹⁄₃₂-in (0.8-mm) silver wire around a ⁵⁄₆₄-in (2-mm) object and cut off three rings. You should now have three ¼-in (6-mm) rings, four ⅛-in (3-mm) rings, and three ⁵⁄₆₄-in (2-mm) rings.

17 Cut one length of the ¹⁄₁₆-in (2.5 mm) round silver wire to make the T-bar. You now have your pieces for the clasp, shown top in the photograph. (The assembled clasp is shown below in the photo; see steps oveleaf for assembly instructions.)

18 Assemble the clasp using parallel pliers to help you close the jump rings. They must be touching, so hold them up to the light to make sure that you cannot see a gap and, using the solder torch and bricks, solder all the rings closed with solder paste. Be careful to not let the solder join the jump rings to one another.

19 Then, using solder paste again, solder the clasp to the ends of the main pieces.

20 Attach the two large jump rings made from ³⁄₆₄-in (1.2-mm) wire to the shaped loop, closing them using the two pairs of parallel pliers.

21 Hold the rings up to the light to check that there is no gap between the two ends. Using a small piece of easy solder on the end of the ³⁄₈-in (10-mm) lengths of ¹⁄₁₆-in (1.5-mm) wire, solder them onto the joint. The solder should have run across the opening so that the joint then disappears.

22 Clean all the silver parts in the acid bath.

23 Clean up any untidy solder joints with a fine file and rubber polishing mops fitted on a micromotor.

24 Rub up the silver with the silver cloth.

25 Drill a hole ¹⁄₁₆-in (1.5-mm) wide and ³⁄₈-in (10-mm) deep into the ends of your wood piece where you want to attach the silver parts.

26 Brush the ebonizing solution onto your sandblasted wood and leave to dry.

27 Once dry, seal the wood with microcrystalline wax, applying it with fine steel wool which won't get caught on the rough surface.

28 Darken the silver parts using an oxidizing solution as directed on the bottle.

29 Once the waxed wood is dry, push the two silver pegs into the holes and then try the necklace on one last time to check that the length is correct and that the clasp is working.

30 Once you're happy with the length, roughen the surface of the pegs and glue down into the holes using two-part epoxy glue, making sure that all of the peg is hidden. Leave to dry.

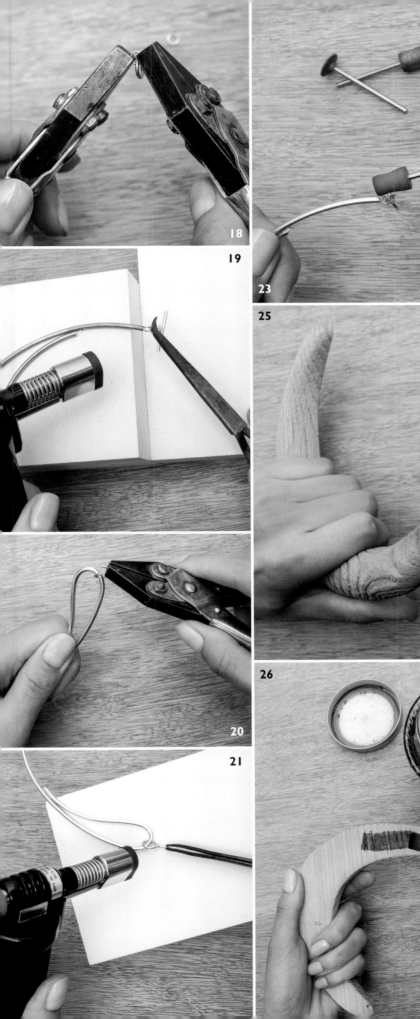

18

19

20

21

23

25

26

27

28

29

Surface finishes

The decision to seal unfinished wood alone is a fairly straightforward choice of aesthetics balanced with practicality. Your choice of sealant is more complicated if your jewelry has been colored because then the sealing layer must not disturb the layer of color below it. Water-based pigments raise the wood grain, therefore, you may need to sand painted surfaces lightly and add another coat. There are also differing opinions on how secure water-based versus spirit-based pigments are for use in jewelry, depending on what the piece of jewelry is and how much it might come into contact with water or perspiration. Some jewelers use acrylic paints sealed with microcrystalline wax without problems and others will only use spirit-based paints. Some makers like a naturalistic look and others like something more artificial, so your choice will depend on the type of effect you are seeking to achieve. Whatever pigment and sealers you choose, a process of experimentation and testing will be needed to develop your own successful pieces. Here, I show a selection of surface treatment experiments I made.

Colored surfaces

A Paint with oil paint thinned with denatured alcohol. Seal with spray varnish; it could also be sealed with a wax.

B Texture with a lino cutter and ball burr, then paint with white acrylic paint. Once dry, sand the surface on a piece of fine sandpaper laid flat on bench. Seal with microcrystalline wax.

C Apply two layers of different-colored acrylic paint to shaped wood. Once dry, run sandpaper over the surface for a distressed look. Seal with microcrystalline wax.

D Acrylic paint; seal with microcrystalline wax.

E Stick stationery stickers onto wood before painting with silver acrylic ink. Once the ink is dry, remove the stickers and seal with microcrystalline wax.

F Use acrylic ink on zebrano wood to allow the wood grain to show through. Once dry, seal with microcrystalline wax.

G Give the wood an undulated texture using the round end of a belt sander. Paint with acrylic ink and rub fine sandpaper lightly over the surface. Seal with microcrystalline wax.

H Paint acrylic ink onto wood, and then once dry, remove some areas with a lino-cutting tool.

I Enamel model-making paint. This is spirit-based and doesn't need sealing, but does need a primer coat and will show any dust left on the wood surface. Available in matte and gloss finishes.

Stained surfaces

Wood stains are available from wood suppliers, usually in brown tones relating to different wood colors. They are available in spirit- and water-based versions and often are sold alongside sealing products. Here, a commercial stain selection: **J** teak, **K** Victorian mahogany, **L** light oak; **M** dark oak, **N** yew, **O** antique pine.

TOOLS AND MATERIALS

- Wood
- Image or text to transfer from a laser printer
- Acetone
- Cotton ball or a paper towel
- Latex gloves
- Wax or clear varnish

Transferring images or text onto wood

There are several ways to transfer images or text onto wood. There are water-based methods but I found acetone, although an unpleasant liquid, less messy. One big advantage of using acetone is that it doesn't warp thin woods. You need to experiment with the density of text to make sure that you get a strong transfer. Use the horizontal flipping tool on your computer to get a mirror image so that the transferred text reads the right way around. The results will vary depending if you use an ink-jet printer, laser printer, or a photocopy machine.

1 Prepare your image or text by printing or photocopying it onto a piece of paper. Here, I have used my signature stamp.

2 Position your image or text onto your piece of wood face down.

3 Working in a well-ventilated room and wearing latex gloves, rub the back of the image or text paper with a cotton ball or paper towel soaked in acetone, being careful not to move your piece of paper.

4 After a minute or so, carefully lift off the paper. The ink should have transferred onto the wood.

5 Seal the result with a clear varnish or wax.

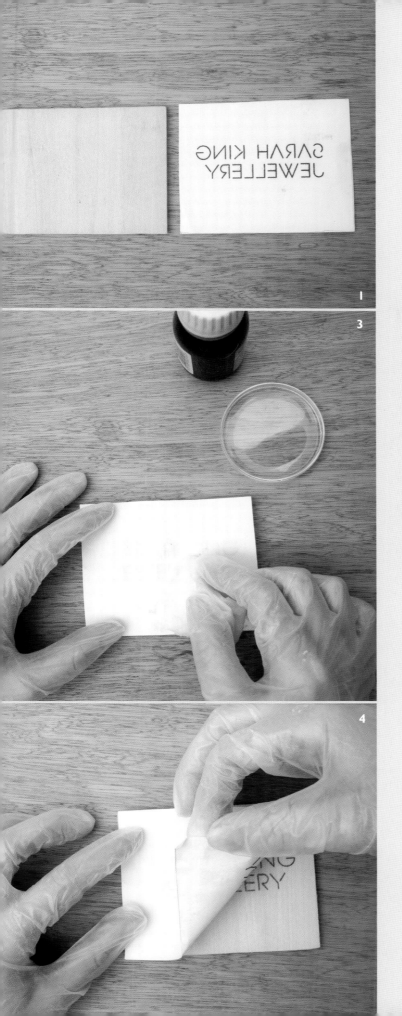

tips

- Try out the text or image you want to transfer on a wood scrap before you work on the actual piece; you should test your chosen sealer, too.

- This method is a good way to apply an outline to wood that you can then use as a guide for your pyrography, inlay, or stitching work.

- You could use this method to apply a commemorative message for a birthday, wedding, or other special occasion.

- The transfer method works best when you use black-and-white ink-jet copies; though some color prints may work, others will not transfer easily.

Ebonizing

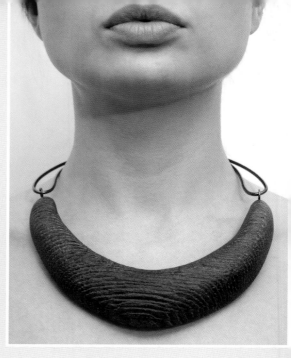

Iron acetate stains woods darker and makes them look like ebony. The solution reacts with tannin in wood so hardwoods with high tannin levels change color much more dramatically than softwoods. Oak, cherry, and walnut work well, but many paler woods do not. Ebonizing needs to be the last stage of a project, before you seal the wood. Be sure to use scraps to check how the stain looks before painting your finished piece. Also test whatever sealing layer you want to finish your piece with to check how the two finishes work together.

TOOLS AND MATERIALS

- Wood for staining
- Fine steel wool
- Cider vinegar
- Liquid detergent
- Airtight jar
- Coffee filter
- Large plastic bottle
- Bowl
- Brush
- Wax or varnish

USING EBONIZING

An ebonized version of the Oak Strata Necklace (p. 142) is shown above right. You could use the treatment on a less expensive hardwood in place of ebony for the Concave Ebony and Pearl Ring (p. 36), but seal the ring before attaching the pearl as pearls are porous. The treatment will also work well on the Walnut Squiggle Pendant (p. 20).

1 Wash your steel wool in hot water and liquid detergent to remove surface oils. Pop the steel wool into the jar with the vinegar and leave it for a week with the lid on. After seven days, the vinegar should have turned black and the steel wool should be dissolved.

2 Cut the top off the plastic bottle and turn it upside down with the coffee filter inserted. Pour the ebonizing solution through the filter into a bowl or jar to remove any residue.

3 It is easier for the solution to soak into the wood if it is not too finely sanded. You may also want to do a pre-ebonizing grain raise by brushing on a little water and leaving the wood to dry before sanding off any whiskers.

4 Paint the solution onto wood test pieces before painting your final piece. In the step 4 photo opposite, the effect is shown on a range of woods. Top row, left to right: Boxwood, sequoia, cedar, oak, pine. Bottom row, left to right: Cherry, walnut, ash, birch plywood, maple.

5 If you want to make the staining darker, brush strong tea onto your wood and then paint over the ebonizing solution while the stained wood is still damp.

6 Paint your final piece; leave it to dry. Once dry, seal it with your chosen wax or varnish. Here, a close-up section of ebonizing on the Oak Strata Necklace (see pp. 142–7) is shown.

Electroforming

TOOLS AND MATERIALS

- Found natural tree product such as a leaf or twig
- Silver jump ring
- Cyanoacrylate glue
- Lacquer or varnish
- Graphite-conductive specialist paint
- Electroforming kit or specialty service

USING ELECTROFORMING

You can use your silvered natural objects on their own as pendants or earrings, or you can incorporate them in a necklace as beads. See the work of Terhi Tolvanen on pp. 104–7 for further inspiration.

You can turn natural items, including parts of a tree, into parts for jewelry using the electroforming process. You need to seal the objects with lacquer and coat them with conductive paint before suspending them in a solution containing metal particles. An electrical current is then run through the solution and the metal particles will coat the object. Home kits are available online and through local retailers. However, beginners should use an electroplater to do the work for them until they are sure that they want to make that financial investment in their own equipment. The challenge with this process is to make it your own, as nature is almost too perfect. You could think about ways to make it unexpected by combining your object with other materials in an unusual way.

1 Dry out your objects by keeping them indoors for a few weeks. Here, I chose a hawthorn twig, a willow leaf, an acorn, and a sycamore seed.

2 Once the items are fully dry, attach a silver jump ring to your pieces using cyanoacrylate glue.

3 Seal the natural objects with several layers of lacquer or varnish.

4 Paint the objects with graphite-conductive paint.

5 Follow the instructions on your kit or send your objects to your electroforming service to apply a thick layer of copper, which is then covered with the layer of silver.

OPPOSITE A selection of finished silvered natural forms created using the electroforming process.

1

2

3

5

Tools and Materials

Measuring and marking

Accurate measuring and marking at every stage is essential for a professional result. Take your time and check your measurements carefully, because once you have cut your material, it isn't easy to correct any mistakes.

RULER
A steel ruler that is marked in both imperial and metric measurements is preferable.

VERNIER CALIPER
This measuring device is more precise than a standard ruler. It is useful for measuring round objects, as the jaws can be secured on either side of an object's circumference.

SQUARE ANGLE
This tool enables you to mark an accurate 90-degree angle.

DIVIDERS
Consisting of a pair of compasses, you can use this technical drawing instrument for marking out circles or arcs. They are also useful for checking the width of something in comparison with another.

GREASE PENCIL OR CHINAGRAPH MARKER
A non-scratch grease pencil will mark clearly on many surfaces. They are resistant to moisture and fading. Remove the marks by rubbing with kitchen towel. A white grease pencil or chinagraph marker is particularly useful for seeing lines drawn on wood.

RIGHT Left to right: ruler, dividers, Vernier caliper, square angle, white grease pencil.

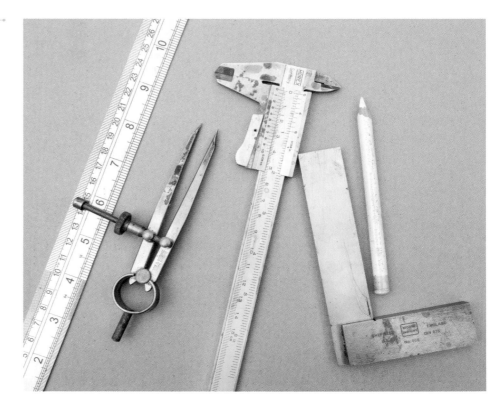

Setting up a workbench

CHAIR
Make sure that you have a comfortable chair that supports your back and is height-adjustable.

BENCH PEG AND ANVIL
The bench peg screws onto the edge of your workbench or table. It consists of a flat steel top that serves as the anvil and a wooden peg or pin that supports pieces while you work on them.

LIGHTING
It is important to have good lighting on your workbench area from a desk lamp with a daylight bulb.

ABOVE Beginner's workbench designed for jewelry-making.

WORKBENCHES
If you have space for a dedicated workbench in a spare room, a garden studio or shed, or garage, then you will find jewelry-making much easier. Benches designed for jewelers are higher than a regular workbench to prevent stooping. They usually have a wooden retaining surround and a leather bench skin on the curved cut-out area designed for ease of working at the front of the bench, so that small parts don't fall on the floor. If you don't have a workbench, then a table with a bench peg secured with a C-clamp will work as an alternative.

ABOVE A bench peg is essential for supporting pieces while you work on them.

Drilling

Drills are essential for making holes in wood and silver. Take care to follow all safety precautions (see p. 167) when working with these sharp tools.

MICROMOTOR

A micromotor is a convenient small drill with interchangeable bits that can be used for a wide range of uses. It plays the same role as a drill press but is more convenient if you don't have a workbench. It is lighter to hold than other DIY drills that sometimes only fit the bits from the same brand.

DRILL BITS

You will need a range of small twist drills with a shank; these are sold in jewelry suppliers.

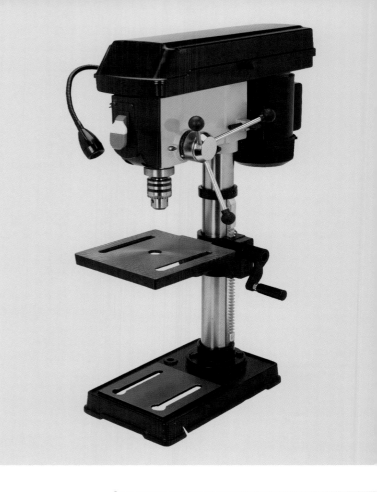

ABOVE A drill press is more accurate than a handheld drill if you have space.

CENTER PUNCH

Use this to mark the hole position before drilling metal. A pen is an easier tool to use on wood.

DRILL PRESS

Also known as a pillar, pedestal, pendant, or bench pillar drill, this bench-mounted piece of equipment is more accurate than a handheld drill. It consists of a column, adjustable-height table, pillar, spindle, and drill head, plus optional accessories and attachments. If you don't have workshop space for a press, you may be able to get access to one at a community or college workshop. They will provide safety training before you use it, but if you are buying your own, be sure to follow all the safety instructions outlined in the manual.

I used a drill press to drill consistently accurate center holes in the square beads for the Oak Broken Line Necklace (see p. 108). The beads were held in one hand and the drill head lowered with the other. The design of a drill press makes it easier and quicker to make 90-degree holes. A bench drill press is fine for small holes, but a larger drill press is better for drilling a large hole in dense wood such as a finger-size hole in ebony. The drill press would make drilling the hole in the Concave Ebony and Pearl Ring (see p. 36) easier.

ABOVE A handheld micromotor drill.

Filing

Files are used for smoothing rough edges on wood or metal. They have detachable handles and come in a range of sizes.

ROUGH AND FINE CUTS

The cut of a file is determined by the number of teeth it has. Files are sold by cut, where number 0-cut is very rough, and a 4-cut fine.

RIFLER FILE

A rifler file has a curved cutting surface for accessing areas that are difficult to reach with a straight file. I have only used it on the Concave Ebony and Pearl Ring project (see p. 36).

HALF-ROUND FILE

Half-round files are the most versatile shape, with one rounded side and one flat side, so if you are only buying one file, then you should select this shape.

NEEDLE FILES

Needle files are smaller files and come in a range of different profiles. They are useful for getting into smaller areas.

WAX-CARVING FILE

A large wax-carving file is sold for carving hard wax, but can also be useful for carving wood.

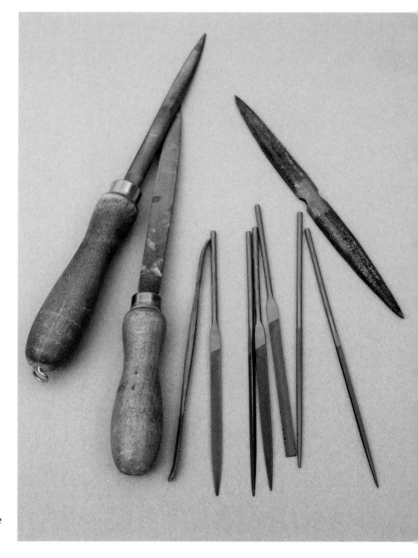

ABOVE Left to right: Rough and fine files, rifler, file, needle files, half-round wax file.

Cutting, hammering, and bending

Saws and cutters are essential to cut both wood and silver wire or silver sheet. You will need hammers and mallets to shape and form metals. Make sure that you follow all safety precautions (see p. 167) when working with these tools. Pliers are used for gripping, twisting, and bending jewelry parts—from closing jump rings to making twisted wire.

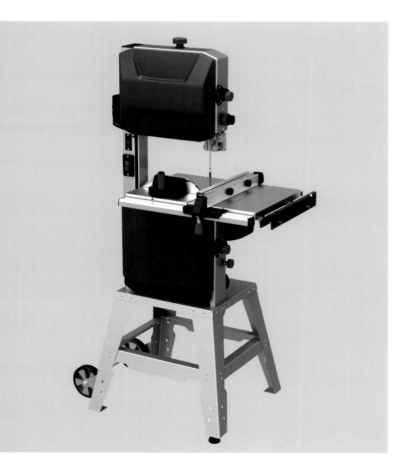

ABOVE A band saw. This model has wheels so you can move it around a workshop.

PIERCING SAW

Interchangeable toothed blades for cutting either metal or wood are held by screws in the saw frame. If the blade starts to stick, use beeswax to ease it or replace it with a new blade.

BAND SAW

Ideal for cutting curves and irregular shapes, a band saw will make a very even, smooth cut. The equipment consists of a table that supports the work under a thin, rotating, toothed band (the saw's blade) that is held in a pair of wheels and powered by a motor. I used a band saw for speed and the accuracy when cutting beads for the Oak Broken Line Necklace (see p. 108), the shaped wood piece for the Oak Strata Necklace (see p. 142), and for cutting the Horse-Chestnut Burr Pin. (see p. 96).

If you don't have workshop space for a band saw, you may be able to get access to one at a community or college workshop. They will provide safety training before you use it, but if you are buying your own, be sure to wear safety clothing (gloves, goggles, and mask) and follow all the safety instructions outlined in the manual.

SNIPS

Also known as shears, use this tool for cutting wire and sheet metal. I also used them to cut the willow and cane for the twisted items.

END CUTTING PLIERS

Use these nippers for cutting silver wire from the top rather than from the side.

ABOVE Left to right bottom: riveting hammer, rawhide mallet, metal hammer, parallel pliers, round-nose pliers, half-round pliers, punch stand. Left to right top: bench block or flat plate, doming block, punches.

SCALPEL AND SCISSORS

You will need a scalpel or utility knife and scissors along with paper, cardstock, and a pencil for making templates. Also, I used a scalpel for carving corks into beads.

BALL BURR

Use a spherical-shaped metal burr in a micromotor to create concave cuts or to shape and hollow out an area.

RIVETING HAMMER

This is a small hammer with one flat round end or face, and the other face with a long ridge or cross-peen, used for driving in rivets and beating metal.

RAWHIDE MALLET

The rawhide head of this mallet produces a gentler impact than a wooden-headed mallet for shaping or flattening metal.

BENCH BLOCK

This steel plate or block is used to hammer against. If you use a metal hammer against it, you will stretch the metal, while if you use the rawhide mallet against it, you will flatten the metal without stretching it.

DOMING BLOCK

Use this solid metal block with punches to bend flat, round discs into domed shapes.

PARALLEL PLIERS

Also known as parallel-action pliers, these tools have a box joint system that enables the round, tapered jaw and flat jaw to stay parallel to each other, providing even pressure across the work. They are really helpful for bending 90-degree angles in wire and making wire straight, and for holding work securely.

ROUND-NOSE PLIERS

The round, tapering jaws of these pliers are useful to put curves into wires.

HALF-ROUND PLIERS

These pliers have one rounded side and one flat side to the jaws. They are useful to bend larger curves, as the rounded side doesn't dig into the silver.

Woodturning

A bench lathe is essential to turn and shape wood. Take care to follow all safety precautions (see p. 167) when working with a power lathe. Chisels are used with lathes to cut and carve wood during the shaping process.

BENCH LATHE

The equipment consists of a fixed lathe mounted on a workbench and powered by a motor. The piece to be worked on is attached to the machine and is then rotated, or turned against a tool to cut, drill, or shape it. I used a bench lathe for the Sycamore Asymmetric Bangle (see p. 60). If you don't have workshop space for a bench lathe, you may be able to get access to one at a community or college workshop. They will provide safety training before you use it, but if you are buying your own, be sure to wear safety clothing

(gloves, goggles, and mask) and follow all the safety instructions outlined in the manual.

FLAT CROSS-CUT CHISEL

Flat chisels are the most common type of chisel. Cross-cut versions have blades that narrow behind the cutting edge to give clearance when cutting grooves and slots.

SKEW CHISEL

With a cutting edge at a 60-degree angle to the axis of the tool, these chisels are used for smoothing, paring, and finishing wood.

GOUGE

A gouge is a chisel with a concave blade.

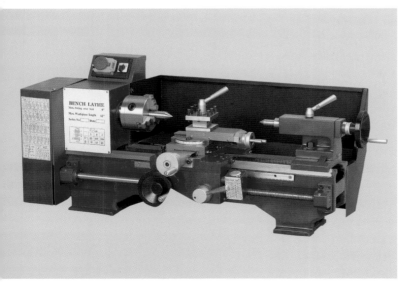

ABOVE A bench lathe.

Sanding and polishing

Sanding machines are essential to sand large areas of wood, and to produce a really smooth surface. Take care to follow all safety precautions (see p. 167) when working with these tools. For smaller areas, handheld wet-and-dry paper will suffice.

WET-AND-DRY PAPER
The grit number denotes the fineness of the paper, from rough 240- or 320- grits to the finer 600-, 800-, 1000-, and (the finest)1200-grit. Wet-and-dry paper can be used to sand both wood and metal.

BELT SANDER
The motor powers a pair of drums supporting a continuous loop of sandpaper, enabling faster and smoother sanding of wood surfaces. A dust-collection system collects the sawdust produced. I used a belt sander to create a smooth wood shape for the Oak Strata Necklace (see p. 142) and for the Concave Ebony and Pearl Ring (see p. 36).

If you don't have workshop space for a belt sander, you may be able to get access to one at a community or college workshop. They will provide safety training before you use it, but if you are buying your own, be sure to wear safety clothing (gloves, goggles, and mask) and follow all the safety instructions outlined in the manual.

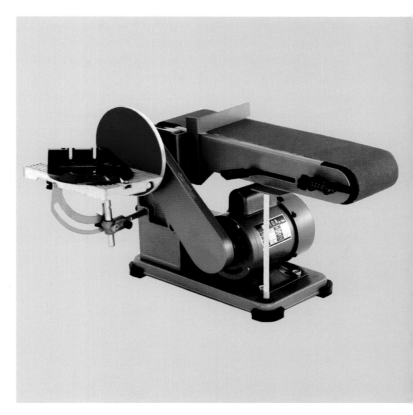

ABOVE A belt sander. If you are working with a lot of wood, attach a vacuum hose to your belt sander and have a general dust extractor in the room.

Soldering

Using heat and a solder material, soldering is the process of fusing two pieces of metal by heating and melting a metal alloy compound, known as solder, to create a joint. Solder is always of a lower melting point than the metals it is joining. When soldering two pieces of silver together, they need to be heated to the same temperature. The silver should be just beginning to look cherry red. Remove the flame if it begins to look too glowing or the metal will melt. With any piece that needs soldering more than once, start with the solder with the higher melting points and work down so that one joint doesn't melt before the next one is attached.

SOLDER TORCH

A hand solder torch for home use powered by butane lighter fuel.

SOLDER BLOCKS

Made from asbestos replacement material, these brick-shaped blocks can be used singly or together to protect adjacent surfaces from the heat of the torch.

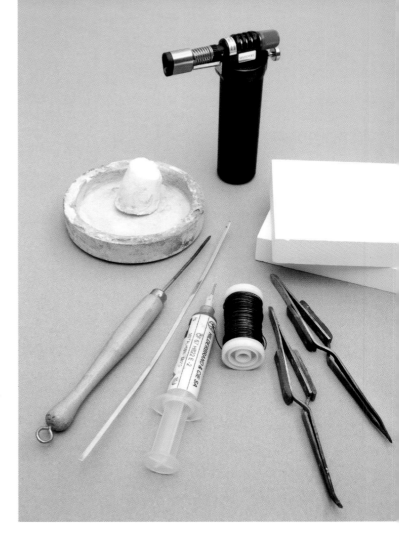

ABOVE Clockwise from top: soldering torch, bricks, reverse-action tweezers, binding wire, solder paste, solder strip, solder probe, borax flux.

soldering safely

It is essential to follow safety precautions when soldering:
• Work in a well-ventilated room
• Clear your working area before you start
• Have a fire extinguisher at hand
• Wear protective goggles and mask
• Tie long hair back, remove dangling jewelry or scarves, cover bare arms and legs, wear shoes that cover all your feet
• Follow the manufacturer's instructions for your torch
• Turn the torch off immediately after you finish using it, and be aware that the tip will still be hot

SOLDER PASTE OR STRIP

Solder is a metal alloy compound and comes in the form of a paste or strip in a range of melting points in the different metals—choose one that contains the metal you are soldering. Silver solder paste has the flux that is needed to help your solder flow already added and is simple to use. You can buy easy or hard versions; these have different melting points. Easy paste is useful for small wire joints, but it isn't good for large jobs because it is not as strong. If you are soldering more than one joint in close proximity, you will need to use different versions, starting with hard solder for the first joint to prevent the heat applied to the second joint reflowing the first one.

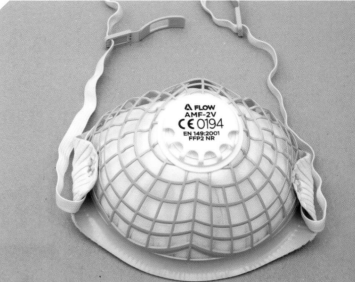

FLUX

The mineral borax cleans the surface of the metal, helping the solder flow. You apply it with a fine watercolor brush and use it with strip or sheet solder.

REVERSE-ACTION TWEEZERS

The closed points on these tweezers open when you squeeze on the handles and grip when released. You will need these to hold the item that you are soldering.

SOLDER PROBE

A solder probe is useful for moving solder to a desired position if it moves as the metal heats up.

BINDING WIRE

A very soft wire for tying pieces together prior to soldering; it won't stick to your solder and is easy to remove once you have made the solder joint.

MASKS

Masks are either designed for dust or fumes or both. Make sure that you are wearing the right one for the job. Spend a little more to purchase one with a valve, as it will be more effective.

general safety advice

Before you take on any project it is essential that you take steps to protect yourself and your work area and are fully aware of all the safety concerns. Make sure that you read the manufacturer's instructions for any tools, chemicals, and other products that you are using.

PROTECT YOURSELF

- Safety goggles protect your eyes from heat and flying fragments of wood or metal
- A mask will protect your airways from chemical fumes and wood shavings or dust. Respirators are more comfortable than they look and are more effective than a basic dust mask
- Wear latex gloves when using chemicals
- Wear simple clothing with nothing that can get caught in equipment and cover bare arms, legs, and feet
- Wear an apron to protect your clothing

PROTECT YOUR WORK AREA

- Have a fire extinguisher nearby
- Make sure that your area is well-ventilated
- Have a clear area on and around your work surface so that there is nothing nearby that can catch fire or be damaged by spilled chemicals
- If you are using a kitchen table, make sure that it is covered with a dedicated plywood board or fire-resistant cloth so that food isn't contaminated later
- When you rinse off chemicals, work in a bowl or sink that is not used for food preparation

Bibliography

The Art of Wood Jewelry
Terry Taylor
Lark Books
ISBN: 978-1-60059-106-8

Contemporary Jewellers
Roberta Bernabei
Bloomsbury
ISBN: 978-1-8452-0769-4

Jewellery from Natural Materials
Beth Legg
A&C Black
ISBN: 978-0-7136-8276-2

Hot and Cold Connections
Tim McCreight
A&C Black
ISBN: 978-0-7136-8758-3

The New Jewelry: Trends & Traditions
Peter Dormer & Ralph Turner
Thames and Hudson
ISBN: 0-500-27774-5

Wood
Chris Lefteri
Rotovision
ISBN: 2-880046-645-8

Woodturning Jewellery
Hilary Bowen
Fox Chapel Publishing
ISBN: 978-1-56523-278-5

Visit
*www.FoxChapelPublishing.com/
suppliers* to find resources.

Useful information

ARTS
American Craft Council
www.craftcouncil.org

Art Jewelry Forum
www.artjewelryforum.org

Contemporary Jewelry Design Group
https://cjdg.jewelry

Klimt02
www.klimt02.net

WoodWorks
www.woodworks.org

ENVIRONMENTAL/TECHNICAL
American Hardwood Guide
www.americanhardwood.org

**Convention on International Trade in
Endangered Species of Wild Fauna and
Flora (CITES)**
www.cites.org

Forest2Market
www.forest2market.com

Forest Stewardship Council
www.us.fsc.org

U.S. Lumber Coalition
https://uslumbercoalition.org

Wood Database
www.wood-database.com

Selected jewelers using wood

Manami Aoki
manami-aoki.wixsite.com

Nutre Arayavanish
www.nutrejeweller.com

Sara Barbanti
www.sarabarbanti.com

Maria Cristina Bellucci
www.mcbjewellery.com

Liv Blavarp
www.charonkransenarts.com

Adele Brereton
www.adelebrereton.com

Susan Chin
www.susanchin.com

Sharon Church
www.sharonchurchjewelry.net

Daniel DiCaprio
www.dandicaprio.com

Hayley Grafflin
www.hayleygrafflinjewellery.co.uk

Katy Hackney
www.katyhackney.com

Joo Hyung Park
www.parkjoohyung.com

Mette Jensen
www.orro.co.uk

Emily Kidson
www.emilykidson.com

Dongchun Lee
www.themaker.kr

Jasmin Matzakow
www. jasminmatzakow.de

Naomi McIntosh
www.naomimcintosh.com

Bruce Metcalf
www.brucemetcalf.com

Yutaka Minegishi
www.yutakaminegishi.com

Helga Mogensen
www.helgamorgensen.com

Kelly Munrow
www.kellymunrojewellery.com

Lena Olson
www.lenaolson.se

Nina Morrow
www.ninamorrow.com

Annika Petersson
www.annikapetersson.se

Dorothea Pruhl
www.dorothea-pruehl.de

Anthony Roussel
www.anthonyroussel.com

Jane Sedgwick
www.janesedgwick.co.uk

Holly Stant
www.hollystant.com

Catherine Truman
www.catherinetruman.com.au

Julia Turner
www.juliaturner.com

Linda van Niekirk
www.lindavanniekerk.com

Francis Willemstijn
www.willemstijn.com

Cristina Zani
www.cristinazani.com

Index

Index of project difficulty and variations

EASY

Walnut Squiggle Pendant

For project, see p. 20

The project could be made more three-dimensional by incorporating stapled or riveted layers. Be careful to distribute the weight of additional parts so that it still hangs well.

Undulating Lime Earrings

For project, see p. 26

You could paint these carved earrings with some of the color experiments on pp. 148–9. The shaping of these earrings could be made more three-dimensional by starting with deeper wood.

Ply Leaf Chain Riveted Necklace

For project, see p. 88

This technique is not hard as long as you do not find CAD drawing a barrier. If you do find this difficult, play around cutting the ply by hand. You could make more complex designs by making slots on your shapes and combining them to make more three-dimensional designs.

Ebony Silver Dot Pendant

For project, see p. 120

The shallow wood is easy to shape and these small pique dots easy to do. You could play around with more three-dimensional shaping in conjunction with silver line inlay, which is harder to do, especially on a rounded surface or around a corner.

Spalted Beech Saucer Stud Earrings

For project, see p. 50

These earrings could be used at a base for silver inlay or colored surfaces.

Twisted Cane Set

For project, see p. 48

This project has an inbuilt variation of difficulty, with the cane being easy and the willow version medium.

MEDIUM

Twisted Willow Set

For project, see p. 42

Try the easier version of the necklace and earrings using cane (see Twisted Cane Set above) first.

Concave Ebony and Pearl Ring

For project, see p. 36

The ring could be made easier by using a less dense wood. Variations could be done by pegging in sheet on the top (in a similar way to the striped cuff links) or putting gilding textures into the top (similar to the bog oak bangle).

Beech Spoon Necklace

For project, see p. 74

This idea could be made simpler by using a single spoon to make a pendant, rather than a whole necklace. You could shape the handle and put on a domed pendant fastening, shown as an alternative for the spalted beech earrings project.

Bog Oak and Maple Striped Cuff Links

For project, see p. 82

The actual laminating of woods is very easy, so start with this and make a pegged pendant fastening instead of the custom back shown on this project The neat fitting of the silver sheet and the crisp shaping of the wood makes this more challenging, so that could be tackled next. You could then cut the wood at an angle to get diagonal stripes, or cut the wood and glue it back together at right angles to make the stripes form more of an L-shaped configuration.

Bog Oak Gold Spot Bangle

For project, see p. 132
My design is an oval bangle, but making a round one would be easier, especially if you use a template. The gilding could be replaced by gold acrylic paint. You could develop this project by making more ambitiously shaped bangles.

Oak Strata Necklace

For project, see p. 142
The scale of the wood that needs shaping in this project makes it a bit harder if you just have jewelry tools. The actual technique is not hard if you have access to woodworking equipment. The silver parts could be made easier by attaching the pin going into the wood to a chain instead. The design could be varied by linking multiple pieces of wood together—you could use links similar to the ones shown in the beech spoon necklace.

HARD

Sycamore Asymmetric Bangle

For project, see p. 60
This is a project for those with woodturning experience, and anyone starting this project without it would want to do a class or seek information specifically for beginners.

Horse-Chestnut Burr Pin

For project, see p. 96
The multiple soldering in this clasp is challenging and you would need to have some silver soldering experience. It would be easier if you had a piece of wood that was a suitable shape to be held with three or four claws. Alternatively, you could pin the back into the wood. If you drilled holes into your silver frame and pushed silver wires into them, they would be held into position for soldering.

Oak Broken Line Necklace

For project, see p. 108
The hidden magnetic clasp makes this project hard. You could simplify it by making your beads and use the crimping method to attach them to a simpler clasp. The variations for the shaping of beads, the types of wood used, the direction of drilling, and their surface decoration, are endless.

Credits

Fil Rouge Press would like to thank Beppe Kessler (*www.beppekessler.nl*), Inni Parnanen (*www.inni.fi*), Lina Peterson (*www.linapeterson.com*), and Tehri Tolvanen (*www.tehritolvanen.com*) for their interviews and for supplying photographs of their work.

Author photograph p. 176: Kathryn Martin.

Acknowledgments

Thank you to Judith More for spotting the lack of a book on contemporary wood jewelry and thinking that I was the right person to write it.

Thank you to all the people who were so generous with their knowledge and help:
Jules Ash, Lise Bech, Nick Benjamin, Juliet & Graham Dann, Katherine Fawssett, Alex Kennedy, Charon Kransen, Eleanor Lakelin, Annemarie O'Sullivan, Charlie Palmer, Polly Pollock, Olivia Schlevogt, Robin Sewell, Jeff Turko, Helen van Eyck, and Wenban Smith

About the author

Sarah King studied Fine Art textiles at Goldsmiths' College, University of London, where an anthropology class ignited her interest in jewelry. She has won numerous jewelry awards, such as the Association of Contemporary Jewelry Prize, a scholarship to study with Cristoph Zellweger at Salzburg Summer Academy, and several commendations from Goldsmiths' Craftsmanship and Design Awards. Her work is held in public collections around the world, including Maryland Institute of Art, USA, Crafts Council and British Council, UK, and Museum fur Kunst und Gewerbe in Hamburg, Germany. She has taught at various UK educational establishments, including the Jewelry School at Birmingham City University, London Metropolitan University, and Kent Institute of Art and Design, and has been a mentor on the Crafts Council Hothouse Program and for ChangeActShare.

She was a Lead Artist in the Designing Deptford Charrette, and was commissioned by Creative Process to develop a Public Art commission. She has collaborated with architect Jeffrey Turko on a ceiling installation and industrial designer Amos Marchant on a Selective Laser Sintering bangle.

She teaches specialist short courses in the use of plastics and wood in jewelry at Central St Martins, Morley College, and West Dean.

Find out more about Sarah King at *www.sarah-king.co.uk*.